What an architecture student should know

It's not just you. Every architecture student is initially confused by architecture school—an education so different that it doesn't compare to anything else. A student's joy at being chosen in stiff competition with many other applicants can turn to doubt when he or she struggles to understand the logic of the specific teaching method. Testimony from several schools of design and architecture in different countries indicates that many students feel disoriented and uncertain.

This book will help you understand and be aware of:
- Specific working methods at architecture schools and in the critique process, so you'll feel oriented and confident.
- How to cope with uncertainty in the design process.
- How to develop the ability to synthesize the complexity of architecture in terms of function, durability, and beauty.

This book is about how architects learn to cope with uncertainty and strive to master complexity. Special attention is given to criticism, which is an essential part of the design process. The author, a recipient of several educational awards, has written this book for architecture students and teachers, to describe how each student can adopt the architect's working method.

Key concepts are defined throughout and references at the end of each chapter will point you to further reading so you can delve into topics you find particularly interesting.

Jadwiga Krupinska is Professor Emerita at the School of Architecture, the Royal Institute of Technology (KTH) in Stockholm, Sweden.

WHAT AN ARCHITECTURE STUDENT SHOULD KNOW

JADWIGA KRUPINSKA

TRANSLATION BY SCOTT DANIELSON

Routledge
Taylor & Francis Group

NEW YORK AND LONDON

First published 2014
by Routledge
711 Third Avenue, New York, NY 10017

and by Routledge
2 Park Square, Milton Park, Abingdon, Oxon OX14 4RN

Routledge is an imprint of the Taylor & Francis Group, an informa business

Library of Congress Cataloging-in-Publication Data
Krupinska, Jadwiga.
What an architecture student should know / Jadwiga Krupinska ; translation by Scott Danielson.
-- 1 [edition].
pages cm
Includes index.
1. Architecture--Study and teachng. 2. Architecture students. I. Title.
NA2000.K76 2014
720.71'1--dc23
2013040695

ISBN: 978-0-415-70232-4 (hbk)
ISBN: 978-0-415-70233-1 (pbk)
ISBN: 978-1-315-79793-9 (ebk)

Acquisition Editor: Wendy Fuller
Editorial Assistant: Emma Gadsden
Production Editor: Alanna Donaldson
Cover & Graphic Design: Studio Carolina Krupinska / Cover photo: Linus Kjellqvist
Typeset in Adobe Caslon Pro By Studio Carolina Krupinska

This book has been prepared from camera-ready copy provided by the author.

Acknowledgments

Several people have contributed their knowledge and experience in the completion of this book. My colleagues at the School of Architecture, the Royal Institute of Technology (KTH), and students have given me inspiration in different ways and have been of great help. I especially want to thank Professor Claes Caldenby, Professor Johan Mårtelius, PhD Gertrud Olsson, and architect MAA Per Olsen for their viewpoints and comments in the relatively early stages of the work. My children, Konrad Krupinski and Carolina Krupinska, have been enthusiastic and involved in the whole lengthy process. Konrad Krupinski helped me as an architect, by reading the manuscript several times, providing precisely formulated constructive criticism after each reading. Carolina Krupinska, a graphic designer, established strict quality guidelines and put many hours into photographing, image editing, and book design. I can't thank them enough. I also want to thank architect Scott Danielson for his patient and accurate translation work, Hazel Johnston for proofreading, and librarian Anna Langaard for her assistance in obtaining books from a variety of collections.

Parts of the book have been written during short visits to the beautiful Kavalla, in guest lodging provided by the Swedish Institute at Athens, and on Capri, in one of the San Michele Foundation's fantastic guest houses.

The English version of this book has been published with the support of: ARQ Foundation; FFNS-Foundation SWECO; School of Architecture, the Royal Institute of Technology (KTH); I. and A. Tengbom's Foundation.

Contents

Preface

When I started my architecture studies as a 17-year-old right after high school, everything was new and interesting. I had no problem completing the design and drawing courses and the exams in all of our subjects. But as the years went by, I understood that for me, design was something abstract. It hadn't really touched my soul. Whether that was due to the teaching or my way of thinking is unclear. I also discovered that my husband, a gifted architect, thought in a different manner than me. I called his way of thinking "to think in terms of form", but I realized later that it was more "to think in terms of flexibility". In any case, that was mysterious and difficult to understand. I believe that these observations—to not limit yourself to the abstract, to be inspired, to understand what you're doing when you're thinking design—have given me a great interest in architectural education. During my years as a practicing architect and perhaps foremost through many years of teaching at a school of architecture, these thoughts were my constant companions.

> If "form" was to be a primary category of architecture, then "design" was its necessary accomplice, for "design" is the activity which realizes form, and brings it into the world: as Louis Kahn put it, "Design calls into being what realization—form—tells us". (Louis Kahn)[1]

Critique, as a teaching method, is especially interesting for me. Through the years I've been a critic innumerable times. This always involved the review and criticism of something the student had brought into the world from their innermost being: visions of buildings and environments that simply were not there before.

Did they really know what happened in that process; how they thought in order to succeed with their proposals? Did the teaching help them (if that is at all possible) and if so, how?

Originally I intended to write a book exclusively about critique as a method of teaching, but the uncertainties that students reveal in different studies (see Chapter 1) indicate the need for a wider perspective on architectural education. In order to demonstrate why critique is an essential part of the architect's working method, we need an understanding of the unique aspects of the architectural profession, the uncertainties of that profession, and how the status of the architect has evolved historically (Chapter 2). One should also know what skills the architect needs, and how to think during the design process, i.e. how to reach good design solutions (Chapters 3–6). Following that, there is extensive coverage of critiques and assessment reviews, and subsequently a final discussion (Chapters 7–10).

1 Student uncertainties

Numerous descriptions from different schools of architecture reveal that students have difficulties figuring out what their education is all about. The joy of being chosen in stiff competition among many others can revert to doubt. Many questions arise: Will I make it through the course? Can I live up to my own expectations—and those of others? Does everyone else know more than me? What is actually going on? The transition from the education at high school or other colleges to the one used at an architecture school demands changes. It is rarely explained explicitly that a whole new way of thinking is needed.

Various accounts and results from surveys show that architecture students feel bad because they are worried daily by too many uncertainties. But you can't say that these studies form a scientifically proven universal truth, because they were not set up very systematically or broadly enough. Also, there is no way of knowing the opinions of the students who did not participate. It is, however, thought-provoking that that testimony about the uncertainties of architecture students comes from different parts of the world, during a span of at least 30 years, and both from schools of architecture and landscape architecture.

To start with, it is about reading social codes. Every new social situation requires a certain adaptation, as described in a thesis from Chalmers University of Technology:

I remember how I noticed that my classmates looked completely normal. They seemed to be a collection of average people between 18 and 40 years old. I also noticed that the students in the upper classes did not look normal in the same way. The majority of them had a style I would soon call "architecty". I noted that the

*style did not just include clothing, but instead, a whole concept
that could even encompass—believe it or not—body language,
facial expressions, opinions, and food habits. It really felt like
they had understood something that I had yet to understand.
They were on their way toward becoming real architects while
I often felt like a forlorn guest. They had all the qualities needed
to become something.* (Wingård 2004/2005, 15)

Sooner or later you find your place in, or your relationship to, a new
social group, but understanding what the education is about can
often be more difficult. Swedish architecture students said in surveys
from the 1980s:

*This education is so different; you can't compare it with anything
else. In the beginning, it was almost a shock.*
(Bessman and Villner 1989, 2)

The students' disorientation increases when, in their first few days
at school, they can be asked to forget most of what they have
learned, come into the project studio *"naked"*, and let themselves
be led by those whom they often consider the great authorities—
their teachers.[2]

*I remember feeling very anxious about my early days in the
undergraduate architecture program at Miami University.
I was unsure about the way we were being directed toward
knowledge, although I was willing to trust that there was
a particular design in the minds of our professors…we were
expected to unlearn everything we absorbed in high school
and before.* (Willenbrock 1991, 97)

And it is not just about the projects, but also one's own identity. It
can also be difficult to understand the esoteric terms the teachers
are using.

*Because the first year involves so many artistic assignments, it
was easy to get scared if, like me, you did not have a well-
developed artistic pathos. I was amazed by how calm everyone*

seemed to be when faced by the vaguest assignments, with thousands of possible interpretations. I now know that I was hardly alone. Many of us were extremely nervous. We looked everywhere for clear signals that could guide us in these very difficult creative situations, where no one could say what was right or wrong. I remember being like a sponge, absorbing anything that could make the ground a little more solid. At the same time, I got very tired of no one using clear language, and I still am. (Wingård 2004/2005, 15)

You are more emotionally involved when you're sitting and struggling with a project presentation than if you take an exam and then are done with it. You are much more engaged. You expose yourself—completely! That is the formative part, the creative part. (Bessman and Villner 1989, 2)

It is especially hard to never get the correct answers; to never know if you've got it right or wrong.

It's not just the start of the course that can be difficult. Many uncertainties remain after the third year, as shown in another study. Students can be unsure about what they know (*we're not taught, we have to find the answers ourselves, then guess*), which working methods are available, what the architect's field of knowledge and methods of practice are, what is good and why, unclear goals and unclear project descriptions.

When asked what the worst part of studying architecture is, one woman says:
The uncertainty; because no one can tell me if I did something wrong, I have to constantly question myself: Have I done something right? Am I good enough? Should I quit right now? (Wingård 2004/2005, 104)

However, that which is considered worst is also considered the most positive, according to some of the students who were interviewed.

The best thing about studying architecture is:

*That you are given the freedom to develop your own thoughts.
That you get to "do" something and not just write out what you
know on a sheet of paper. All the practical and creative work!
You plan your own time. There is no right or wrong. You take
responsibility for yourself. More like a workplace than a school...
Openness. You find yourself and get a chance to express yourself.*
(Wingård 2004/2005, 107)

One of the methods of architectural education that many students
have particular difficulty relating to is critique.

*I remember my first desk crit as a landscape architecture student.
I was so proud of the work I had produced. "This was good", I
was thinking to myself. My professor didn't exactly agree. My
intentions were questioned. Feedback was given to me on how
I could change my work in order to take my ideas to the next
level. It took a few minutes to get over my bruised ego and absorb
the criticism that I was given before I could continue working
on my project. Now that I think about it, I was looking for
approval. Instead, I received my first spoonful of criticism.*
(Graham 2003, 2)

Critiques and assessment reviews as educational methods are covered in many survey answers. I will discuss this in more detail in
Chapters 7–9.

Thus there are several aspects that architecture students struggle
with. It is a paradox that many students feel disoriented and in-
secure, just as the architect's working methods are praised internationally as a way of dealing with precisely that: uncertainties.[3]

Notes

References

1 Cited by Forty, 2004 (2000), 136.

2 Willenbrock, L., 1991, 98, 112, my cursives.

3 This interest was sparked by Donald Schön's pioneering work on the role of reflection during practical work. See also Chapter 4.

Bessman, Mona; Villner, Lena: *Mötet med arkitektur. Lärarnas roll i projektundervisningen.* Rapport från det Pedagogiska utvecklingsarbetet vid KTH 1989: 60, 2–3

Forty, Adrian: *Words and Buildings. A Vocabulary of Modern Architecture.* Thames and Hudson 2000, 136

Graham, Elizabeth Marie: *Studio Design Critique: Student and Faculty Expectations and Reality.* A Thesis. The School of Landscape Architecture. Christian Brothers University 2003, 2

Willenbrock, Laura L.: *An Undergraduate Voice in Architectural Education.* In: Dutton, Thomas A (ed.): *Voices in Architectural Education. Cultural Politics and Pedagogy.* Bergin & Garvey, New York 1991, 97–112

Wingård, Lisa: *Om att bli arkitekt* (On Becoming an Architect). In Swedish. Examensarbete Chalmers Arkitektur 2004/2005

2 Professional uncertainties

The architect: a historical overview

As a first step, I want to give an outline of the historical process to approach the questions raised by several students: What is the architectural profession? What is *the architect's role and responsibility in society*? Somewhat simplified, one could say that the development of architecture as a profession has been a tug-of-war with the other forces involved in building and construction. During some periods, the architect's desire for independence, which characterizes creative individuals (see the section entitled "Creative personality" in Chapter 8), has been particularly evident, but not always successful when interacting with the various players in the field of construction.

The concept of *arkhitekton* was already used by Herodotus in the 5th decade BC. The word is a combination of the Greek word *arkhi*—from *archos*, or chief (from the same root as in archbishop)—and *tekton* (master builder). One could say that the word architect means *master of the building arts*, or *chief master builder*. Until recently, this was invariably a man. Traditionally, the architect has always been associated with the rich and powerful, since they were the ones who could afford to build. He had a special position in society, but this did not always mean that he was favored in the social hierarchy. Nevertheless, an architect was not, as Plato describes it, a worker, but was instead the one who actually made the rules for the workers; he supplied knowledge but not the handcraft (Kostof 1977a).

In ancient Egypt he was "the chief (boss) over the foremen" as Ineni, the chief of the workmen in Karnak, was described on a grave inscription. It is not known exactly when the use of drawings was introduced, even though they are now such an integral part of the architectural profession. It is unclear if drawings were used for the plans and building facades in Ancient Greece. The work descriptions that do exist have the character of craftsmen's notes. They describe the quality and size of the stones to be used, and how they are to be stacked.

In Greece and Rome an architect learned partly theory, which at that time meant proportion studies, and partly construction techniques on the building site. There was no clear distinction between architecture, engineering, and urban planning.[1] Therefore the architect's theoretical and practical education occurred simultaneously. According to Vitruvius, an architect should have a multidisciplinary education. An architect's general education included the proper way for a gentleman to socialize and also participation in a professional architectural education (a studio), which was led by a practicing architect. Vitruvius recommends that an architect "has to be able to handle the pen so that he can do quick sketches to illustrate his proposals", but that he should also be good at writing. The graphic convention of classical design included plans (*ichnographia*), to show how the building would be placed on the ground, facades (*orthographia*) and perspective views (*scaenographia*). For the Romans, architecture was both functionally and symbolically more important than the other arts, and an architect was a person of importance. An effective federal organization for financing, materials transport, and supplying workers supported the skill and energy of the architect.

The architectural historian William MacDonald says that the Roman statesman Cicero considered architecture to be equal to the arts of medicine and teaching. While an architect in Greece was, in a sense, the main sculptor among other sculptors, the Roman architects reached heretofore unseen importance and independence by mastering the design and construction of the new discoveries—the arch and the vault.

During the Middle Ages, the architect reached his high position through hard work and natural talent, and not because of an inherited social position (they often came from the lower social classes), according to architectural historian Spiro Kostof. The architect's

In the 16th century, geometry was personified by an elegant, refined woman—with her feminine intuition, creativity, and ability to synthesize, but when geometric rules began to be used in technology and everyday life, geometry was seen as a practical, rational endeavor in the domain of men (Lawlor 1998).

image as an intellectual was reinforced by God being characterized as an "artistic architect" (*elegans architectus*) who created a universe harmonious for all living beings by employing musical proportions. Geometry was of very high status during the Middle Ages because it was thought to be the aesthetic and technical basis for the universe and was placed on the same level as three other liberal arts (*artes liberales*): astronomy, music, and arithmetic. In other words, these were all intellectual pursuits that required theoretical knowledge and specific skills, in contrast to *artes illiberales*—the menial vocational education for the workers. Theoretical knowledge of geometry separated the architect from the master builder—which is why the architect was often shown with geometrical measuring instruments in the haughty portraits of the time.

During the Gothic age, a geometric formula, well chosen by the architect, was considered a guarantee that a building would have the correct design, both in terms of construction and aesthetics. Then, the art of masonry would guarantee that this theoretical construction would be correctly executed.[2] An apprentice system provided career training for new architects. A beginner assisted his master, learned from watching his master work, and was corrected as required when he tried his own skills. The normal time to become a journeyman was seven years, starting at the age of 13 or 14. Following that were three trial years as a subordinate, completing different types of work and travel. The master could not always explain why things were done a certain way, only that they simply would work. Bernhard Tschumi explains: "From the time of Pyramids to the end of the Middle Ages the architect lived on the building site and rarely existed as an independent individual" (1995, 24).

The description above is that of the esteemed position of the architect in the western world. However, if we look further we see, for example, that in pre-modern Chinese society the profession of the architect (as with the craftsman and the engineer) was not very highly respected. Researchers/bureaucrats who were recruited to work in the government agencies were examined according to specific rules and had a considerably higher status than architects. Architectural knowledge was handed down from father to son or to an apprentice in the same way as it was done in the crafts. There were, however, early architectural texts in China with encyclopedic information on traditional architecture, and as early as the 12th century there was an illustrated building handbook.

Practitioner or academic?

Practical experience in *disegno*—essentially drawing and perspective—was the only standard formal training an architect received during his apprenticeship at the start of the Renaissance. Journeys, normally to Rome, were a common aspect of an architect's education. Equipped with perspective drawing and mathematical skills and knowledge of the architecture of Rome, an artist could become an architect. However, the practical focus proved inadequate as a revived interest emerged for the ancient proportional relationships. A tension arose between the interpretation of the timeless principles and the individual master's personal ability to apply them.

In the 15th century a new architectural concept was introduced, derived from classical theory. Leon Battista Alberti presented, in his tract *De Re Aedificatoria*, the ideal of architectural harmony where nothing could be added or removed from the whole without destroying it. To accomplish this, it was necessary to have architects who could be responsible for every part of a building, without necessarily taking part in the actual construction. Alberti added mathematics and painting to the classic Vitruvian model and therefore, according to Johan Mårtelius, a professor of architectural history, he laid the foundation for the architect's dual affiliation—to the academies of the arts and to the science of engineering.

The acceptance of Alberti's theory meant that architecture could not just be learned solely by engaging in practical work at the building site; it also required study. Because of this, the architect acquired both a high status as an educated person and also the freedom to choose the techniques and materials he considered appropriate. Alberti's definition of the architect as a thinking *homo cogitas* diverged from the medieval concept of *homo faber*—the architect as craftsman. This paved the way for the idea that the art of building is dependent on a cultivated and educated way of thinking. As free universal geniuses, architects could express their artistic and intellectual powers.

Thus the mutual dependence between practice and theory had been established, but there was still no formal architectural education. Leonardo da Vinci said that good work in a given field requires fundamental knowledge. Young people should acquire that *before* they start their careers. The first official art academy—Accademia e Compagnia delle Arti del Disegno—was founded in 1563 in Florence, heavily influenced by the architect Giorgio Vasari, who wanted to counteract the separation of practice and theory that Leonardo had criticized. Practical work in the workshops was therefore supplemented by academic training, in that the students worked in their master's studio while three "visitors" chosen by the academy made regular visits to criticize their work based on the principles of the academy. This workmanlike, characteristic, and natural interweaving of theory and practice held sway for several centuries.

The Renaissance image of an architect as an all-powerful designer characterized the profession until recently. The protagonist in Ayn Rand's book *The Fountainhead*, a young, uncompromising architect who pointedly demonstrated his independence, may have reinforced this image. Over six million copies of the book were sold when it was published in the middle of the 1940s. The view of the architect as a universal genius changed when architects began to feel bound by heavy responsibility. The development of industrial building techniques and strong construction companies has probably contributed to the revised image of the architect.

The split between architecture and construction

Changes in the interpretation of the relationship between theory and practice have affected the development of the architectural profession. Of even greater importance were the societal changes that caused the gradual dissolution of the once intimate connection between architecture and construction. Bernard Tschumi has identified three significant rifts in this development that show an ever-increasing gap between architecture and construction: during Antiquity, at the end of the 1800s, and after 1968.

The first split came when the ancient debating academies were replaced by institutions with the character of a university, with teachers and a listening audience, and when academies began to claim ownership of the truth. During the Mannerist Period and later in the Baroque era, the academies triumphed in the struggle with the guilds and won the right to teach art and architecture. The establishment of the first architecture school—Académie Royal d'Architecture—in the France of Louis XIV, in 1670, can be seen as an example of this emerging split between architecture and construction. One group of leading architects wanted the school to teach "a more exact knowledge and more correct theory". However, behind the establishment of the school there was also a political motive, namely that the architects wanted to weaken and free themselves from the guilds that had become so powerful, through statutes that protected the monopoly of the master masons. According to the guild, it was not the architect who would, in the spirit of Alberti, take responsibility for the entire building and the details, but rather the master mason who had total responsibility to his client. The separation of the theoretical aspects of architecture from construction was a way to divide and conquer. The apprentice architect would now be in the classroom, not on the building site. He would no longer build; that would now be done by stone masons and carpenters. In the 18th century there was even a desire to lift the status of the architect to the same level as the philosopher. This tendency to make the architectural profession more academic was enhanced by the teaching that was established by the French "École Royale des Beaux Arts" in 1819 with programs emphasizing drawing and focusing on classical Greek and Roman art and architecture. Subjects like architectural theory, architectural history, structural engineering, perspective drawing, and mathematics were added. Around the year 1900, the program was extended with chemistry, descriptive geometry, and building law, among others. The scientific subjects required examinations.

According to Tschumi, the second split between architecture and construction occurred at the end of the 19th century in conjunction with technical developments in American industry. The introduction of iron and steel frames generated new methods of construction, allowing the industry to begin replacing the architects in defining the building process. A product and its fabrication were no longer part of one cohesive handcraft process. Instead, a gradual transition to industrial manufacturing led to a more abstract design process, because the designer could no longer control the work. Products had to be fully thought out before the design was put into production. The earlier intimate contact with the materials and tools that could be held in one's hands was no longer possible. A patent for reinforced concrete construction, secured by the French entrepreneur François Hennebique, broadened the influence of engineers in the field of construction.

Since then, technical and artistic education, including architectural, has been elevated to university level in most countries. The Architectural Association in London was founded in 1847; ETH in Zurich in 1855, and the École Royale des Beaux Arts became a university in 1863. Despite the Arts and Crafts tradition and attempts by engi-neering schools to mold the education of architects, the teaching methods of the École Royale des Beaux Arts, with their great emphasis on drawing and classical traditions, were very dominant. Theory was taught in the classroom, while design was taught in a completely separate studio, with different instructors. This applied in both Europe and North America. Students started with proportion studies and the classic orders, and then continued with plan drawings. The careful reproduction of historical styles and detailing was paramount. Bauhaus arrived in the 1920s with new ideas on architectural education and the principle of the studio that had been introduced by École Royale des Beaux Arts was further refined. A powerful ideological impulse brought the past and future together, partly through a respect for traditional hand-craft, and partly through an understanding that industry needed design for mass-production. This was combined with the daring artistry of the teachers and the students. The main aim was to create a contemporary style that was appro-priate for the new machine age, by integrating art and technique. Bauhaus was founded on the thought that a new world order, a new society, would be built after the war, with the architect leading the way. The architect was seen as the voice of the people and of the times. The basic methods of the Bauhaus school were derived from the apprentice tradition of the Middle Ages. Teachers were called masters and students were called apprentices or journeymen. On the cover of the Bauhaus manifesto, there is a picture of a medieval cathedral, symbolizing the spirit of camaraderie between craftsmen, artists, and architects.

The new Bauhaus building in Dessau from 1925, designed by Walter Gropius, contained studios for the students' living quarters, a pool, and a gymnasium. Because of this, design education became an integrated world of life, work, and recreation. Education at the Bauhaus was based on the same principles of "learning by doing" that had been expressed earlier by the American philosopher John Dewey. During the first Bauhaus period, they had ideas about a good society and a social utopia involving the social function of art. Emphasis was placed on the importance of collective work, a cooper-ative production process, and student input on the program through a council. To "build" was both a moral and a practical pursuit. The Bauhaus tradition had a great influence on schools of architecture around the world, especially in the USA, since several of the leading Bauhaus teachers, including Walter Gropius and Mies van der Rohe, immigrated to the US from Nazi Germany. In the post-war years, many architects became known as cultural figures who had political influence, particularly with regard to housing issues.

The third split in the development of the architectural profession has, according to Tschumi, grown out of the new social consciousness after 1968. Interdisciplinary interests and attempts to combine art, architecture, film, and linguistic studies encouraged complex architectural projects where "theory" was the keyword. "Theoretical practice" became established as a concept and many younger architects began to focus not on building, but on writing and publishing. Architects became even more estranged from building and the powers that control it. Within the architectural community a gap began to emerge between "star architects" who created design sketches eagerly published by the mass media, and the almost anonymous architectural firms largely engaged in producing construction documents for these spectacular sketches. This is of course an extreme description, as an illustration, because there have been many independent architectural firms that have done good work without worrying about their "star status".

Since Tschumi wrote his text in 1995 there have been dramatic changes, partly because of concerns about climate change and partly because of the new possibilities created by digital media, performative and parametric design, and the architectural profession's increasing involvement in environmental and societal issues. Building material questions came under scrutiny again. The utopian pursuits and provocations of the 1960s and 1970s have been revived at several schools of architecture. As an example, a current project called Radical Pedagogy, led by Professor Beatriz Colomina at Princeton University School of Architecture, is based on the experiments of the 1960s and aims to show how to revolutionize the teaching of architecture. In addition, the internet has given architects the opportunity to achieve a broad, immediate propagation of their ideas by presenting their projects online using current sites such as Dezeen or Arch Daily.

Earlier, the architect was responsible for the entire design process, but an erosion of this tradition has been accepted by architectural organizations in several countries. This trend has been further reinforced by the European Union's directive on the bidding rules for publicly financed large investments which states that design commissions of one single project (over a certain investment level) have to be divided into smaller segments between different architectural firms and between other construction businesses. Presumably, the goal was to promote competition as a means of lowering costs, but the end effect is that the architect is not only separated from construction, but also from holistic design. This is a fragmentation that can be most nearly compared to the absurdity of having, in the interests of competition, several authors write different parts of a novel which is supposed to be a holistic entity. There is a great risk of this procedure leading to architecture that is less well thought out and to lower quality construction with more frequent technical errors. The essential pendulum movement in the design method between the entirety and the details can be lost when the responsibility is split up, both in the design and construction phases.

A genius, administrator, or an engineer of fortifications?

The development of the architectural profession has undoubtedly varied between countries, with different emphases on the artistic, technical, or social scientific aspects. The first school of architecture in the United States was established at the Massachusetts Institute of Technology in 1869. Architectural education in the USA grew out of the École Royale des Beaux Arts tradition as it did in several other countries, but toward the end of the 1920s more and more teachers, students, and practitioners felt that this style of teaching was outmoded. Increasing criticism was directed at the over-emphasis on competition and on design briefs that were neither "humanistic" nor "pragmatic". These changes accelerated when the émigré Bauhaus teachers from Germany became more established at American architecture schools. The Bauhaus pedagogical belief of *learning by doing* had a strong influence. Competitions à la Beaux Arts gradually disappeared, while the drafting studios opened up to a more modern and less formal teaching style, with more cooperation between students. Teachers became more of a partner in the learning process rather than a detached lecturer. Another major innovation was the introduction of the Town Planning Studio at Columbia University, with its emphasis on urban renewal.

The problems of teaching architecture have been highlighted recently in China, where it is apparent that foreign architects often win the architectural competitions that are a part of the enormous pace of construction in that country. Chinese students are eager to learn, to engage critically in architectural discourse, and they are interested in critical thinking, but it is difficult for them to escape the traditional examination system that has been in place for a thousand years, established by the Chinese Empire to test administrators for the government bureaucracy. According to Austin Williams, associate professor at the School of Architecture, Xi'an Jiaotong-Liverpool University (XJTLU), the current teaching at Chinese architecture schools tends to reinforce this tradition. This was discussed during an international symposium in 2009.

In Sweden, the architectural profession has been influenced by two different traditions: partly a strong handcraft tradition of building with wood, which was not so common in the rest of Europe, and partly due to the construction of military fortifications. In France and Germany, architects (for example, Daniel Speckle, who was known as a fortification architect) did, indeed, design enormous fortifications in the 16th century, but the Renaissance ideal of the architect as a classically educated universal genius hardly reached Sweden. While foreign architects were commissioned for qualified design work on palaces, manor houses, and public buildings in the 16th and 17th centuries, a layman in Sweden could actually build his own house in wood, which was a cheap, readily available material. Other architectural work like building design and city planning was done by fortification engineers who also had a certain amount of education in the field of architecture. Beyond this, there was only the apprentice system, supplemented by journeys to Europe's most important architectural centers for the purpose of learning.

Even as late as the 1960s, Swedish architects had more in common with fortification engineers than they did with the artists of the Renaissance, according to the architectural historian Björn Linn. The association with technical universities may have contributed to this. Today, this tradition is not as clear, because the focus of architectural education and the profession has gradually changed. Since the 1970s, the number of subjects has gradually decreased, giving way to studio projects. The hope was to encourage holistic thinking by reducing the impact of subject boundaries. The connection with the tradition of military fortifications has been replaced by an emphasis on form and design. This brings with it an inherent uncertainty because design work is fraught with subjectivity, meaning that there are no "correct" solutions.

Concerns with subjectivity

In the design process there is an inherent subjectivity that is necessary not only to unleash the architect's artistic ambitions, but also to enable professionally accurate choices concerning the relationships between both the parts and the whole, and also aesthetic expression (see also Chapter 5, "The design process"). Depending on which aspects the architect concentrates on, this can give different results. This is very obvious when an entire class of architecture students is given the same design assignment, with the same site and the same program. Usually, there are as many different solutions as there are students. This subjectivity involves a professional challenge, but also uncertainty. You may be sure of your choice, but can you convince others about this? How can the subjective choice be defended during meetings with lay clients or other participants in the building process? The architect's knowledge and field of work, which spans across art, techniques, humanities, and crafts, can potentially generate difficult situations in relation to clients. On the one hand, the hallmark of the architect is artistic ability, but an artist cannot create art that is dictated by a lay client who is artistically ignorant.

On the other hand, there can be, and often are, relevant requirements for the function of the building or environment that can clash with the building's durability or aesthetic expression.

Professional judgment, mixed with subjectivity, can sometimes be considered inferior when confronted with objective, fact-based arguments, even when it is precisely the "correct" solution. The opposite concept, objectivity, is especially difficult in planning because the actual choice of a problem to investigate is not neutral. Measuring methods are not always dependable and the measuring instruments are chosen only because they are readily available. For example, to measure air quality, instruments are used that measure air exchanges, but there are no instruments that can measure smells as well as the human nose. Even so, the word objectivity is used to evaluate different proposals, and it has surprising weight, despite being so elusive. Subjectivity, on the other hand, has a lower status, and therefore has often been camouflaged in different ways. If a solution is presented as objective, it is often shielded effectively from attack.

Powerful doctrines have been used during different periods within the field of architecture to promote various ideologies and viewpoints. Also, these doctrines have probably helped in avoiding the display of these subjective values that are always part of the design process, precisely because they are so difficult to defend. The craft tradition could provide a convincing "fact-based" methodology ("this is how it's done") based on a strong awareness of tools and materials. The other strong tradition originated in antiquity— that beauty is an inherent property which can be formulated based on a collection of rules for proportions. With certain variations, it was possible to use these rules as a kind of measuring stick and a basis for evaluation. Later, the rules began to be seen as limiting, but limitations on the designer's complete freedom were not always a disadvantage. Instead of being infinite, the number of possible design solutions could be reduced. Also, the rules could camouflage the subjective choices that were actually made.

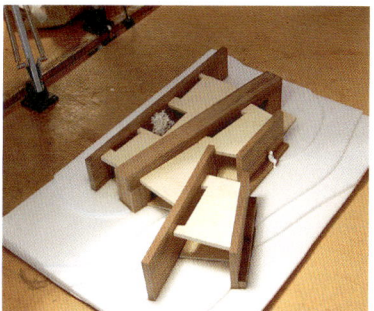

One single assignment—to design a vacation house on the same lot—can result in many different subjective interpretations. Examples of models by students in year 2: Linnea Eriksson, Kajsa Blohm, Lisa Andreasson, and Johannes Hultman. Photo: Katarina Krupinska

Judging by Palladio's submissiveness in the foreword to his *Quattro libri dell'architettura* (1570), the architect's status as a universal genius was not sufficient to sway a client. *Quattro libri* is a practical construction textbook in which Palladio does not discuss *why* a particular proportion is superior to another, but rather he simply states, subjectively, that certain proportional relationships are more beautiful. But the proportions that he used were partly a result of drafting tools and methods which influenced the original design. Professor Olle Svedberg investigated Palladio's work methodology in designing Villa Barbaro in Maser and he ascertained that it was not a process of finding room proportions and *then* adding the rooms together. Instead, it involved general sketches that were revised in accordance with the rules of proportion. Quite possibly, the mystery surrounding beautiful proportions could give the architect authority in relation to the client.

A paradigm shift in the 19th century introduced the view that experiencing art and architecture is a subjective process, different for each individual. This meant that architects were given greater freedom to interpret projects, but at the same time it became more difficult because there was no longer a given standard to relate to. If one person creates something subjectively and another person experiences it subjectively, then judgments will be subjective; greatly influenced by the experiences and sensibility, reached through knowledge and education, of both the creator and the beholder.

Strong styles, like Modernism, led to a reduction in the number of possible solutions, which made it easier to "explain" a chosen form. Problems with subjectivity were parried with doctrines about "honesty" in building design, and also with the need to emphasize the functionality of a building. *Honesty* required that one could read which construction elements were load-bearing and which elements were supported by them. Buildings should manifest themselves without any camouflaging ornament. A more or less constraining viewpoint was that if the building's function was solved logically, then the form and structure would be self-generated. The phrase *form follows function*, coined by Louis Sullivan, became the axiom for Modernist architects.[3] This reductionist view of the art of building coincided with the desire of society and industry to facilitate mass production. The new material—steel-reinforced concrete—and its use by Le Corbusier in Villa Savoye (see image on p. 36) was a showpiece for the rules of Modernist architecture and indicated the direction of the movement, but this did not always match the general aesthetic values of society at large.

If the question of beauty is discussed today, it is seen primarily as a psychological and socio-cultural phenomenon. In principle, it is often seen as "good taste" for an individual or for a group. And taste is difficult to discuss: *De gustibus non est disputandum.*[4] However, the subjective nature of architecture is not only rooted in aesthetic priorities, but also by both the choice of how to interpret a given problem and the choice of a solution that determines the relationship between the details and the whole, among other things. These choices are dependent on the professional judgment that the architect develops during the process of education and architectural practice.

Trying to reduce uncertainties

In earlier times, the architect was in direct contact with the client, who was most often the user of the building, and thus he would get first-hand information on functional, aesthetic, and other preferences. He (and, more seldom, she) could use sketches to establish a dialogue with the client about the building's design. This is still the process used in smaller projects, but the extremely extensive and rapid pace of construction after World War II made it impossible to have a direct dialog with any future residents during the design phase, because there were simply too many of them and the time schedule was too tight. For example, during the post-war period in which Sweden was building 100,000 housing units each year, the authorities became the arbiters. Any direct contact with the people who would live in the buildings was curtailed. The preferences of

Villa Savoye, Poissy, France (completed in 1931) illustrates Le Corbusier's five rules for modern architecture: 1) the house on pilotis, 2) the free facade, 3) the open floor plan, 4) ribbon windows, and 5) a roof garden. Photo: Christian Ahlskog

these future residents were re-evaluated into general terms. The definition of a healthy, functional residence was formulated by recommendations, standards, and codes, and no longer by professional judgment. The powerful social interest that was kindled after 1968 made it imperative to formulate rational and dependable data on people's needs.

Developments in building technology and changes in areas of responsibility have led to a gradual weakening of the architectural profession. In the resistance against this relegation, two different strategies came to the fore: 1) the endeavors to make the design process more scientific in the 1960s; 2) the efforts to promote the importance of intuition and creativity. Modern architectural history can be described by viewing the creative work of the architect as a fluctuation between two poles: rationality and irrationality.

The first of the two—the rational strategy—had political support, and therefore an advantage, while the intuitive direction was more limited to the work of individual architects. Extensive research specifically targeting housing and the working environment was initiated as part of the rational strategy. The goal was to assess the needs and wants of the anonymous users in a scientific way, to establish a reliable basis for the design work. Also, the structuralistic approach revealed the need to find ways to adapt buildings to changes during their life cycle. Concepts like *flexibility* (building adaptability) and *generality* (the possibilities for a building to encompass different activities without changes) were introduced. The design process itself was also investigated and analyzed scientifically in order to systematize it. The next question was: How do designers think and operate when they create new products and environments? The hope was that this new knowledge could be used to rationalize the design process and, eventually, to develop creative computers.

The word "user" was introduced as a design term throughout the English-speaking world in the late 1950s. This concept was used to denote "an average person who uses housing, workplaces, or other buildings". The anonymous character was, as noted, an abstraction, and thus very difficult to define during the period of the welfare state's hectic building program. It was thought that science could provide solutions and assist, not only in better understanding, but also in giving objective accounts of the users' needs. There was a great faith that the planning and design process could be rationalized, following objective and unambiguous descriptions and models.

Within architectural theory, an interest for rational methods arose, and in Sweden the traditions of fortification engineering probably reinforced this viewpoint. In the Sweden of the 1960s and 1970s, there was a strong belief that the architectural profession could be seen as an engineering profession. This view was later criticized by many theorists:

> *An extreme variant of architecture theory maintains that*
> *practical concerns such as economical, technical, and functional*
> *requirements should entirely shape the built environment.*
> *This is not a sustainable position; in fact, there are many*
> *different ways to build with a chosen material or for*
> *a given purpose.* (Caldenby and Walldén 1986, 6)

One methodology that has influenced perception for many years was developed by the architectural theorist Christopher Alexander. The starting point for his so-called Pattern Language was a belief that a program for design can be split up into segments that can be treated individually and then combined into a whole. In fact, this was a hierarchy of sub-systems where each has its own autonomy. These segmented problems, together with one or more proposed solutions, were called patterns, which were illustrated in detail for cities and neighborhoods, houses, gardens, and rooms. The book *A Pattern Language* contains over 250 patterns, for instance, "house cluster", "private terrace on the street", "bathroom" or "front door bench". The idea was that the patterns would be evaluated in discussions with the users and, after corrections, they would be combined into what Alexander hoped were objective wholes. The entire process was supposed to be more transparent and controllable. Such a scientific method seemed at first glance to be irresistible. The Pattern Language signaled changes in the role of the designer, but the method was used very little in real life. Alexander and his colleagues introduced his method in connection with a proposal for a housing project in Lima, Peru, where a system of choosing between 67 general patterns was presented as a way of promoting individual user influence.

In Sweden, Alexander's Pattern Language was used by Johannes Olivegren in designing the Klostermuren housing project for 12 families in Gothenburg. Fixed-price "building blocks", as proposed by the architect, were used as a basis for the planning. The building blocks were assembled during group meetings, in many different configurations. These group meetings were very important. According to Olivegren, the buildings themselves were not to be the main result, but rather the social milieu and the social process that allowed the participants to interact. Olivegren became aware of a large discrepancy in people's reactions to a simulated (preliminary) choice and a real choice. During the simulated choice, people avoided expressing their real wishes if that would risk a conflict with other participating users. During the real choice, the same people would not accept compromises. At that point they would fight for their interests, even if that could cause conflicts.

Several different methods were developed during the 1970s to integrate the users' viewpoints in planning. Examples of these were: field analysis, impact statements, and cumulative programming. Some of these methods bordered on sociology, to the detriment of the identity of the architectural profession. Confusion about terminology was rampant.

The impetus for the new ideas was the publicity surrounding the dramatic demolition of a housing project in St. Louis, Missouri in 1972, just 20 years after it was built. The area was plagued by vandalism and the crime rate was higher than in other areas. The contributing factors to this project having become a slum were thought to be anonymity, long corridors, and the austere style of the buildings—not at all in line with the residents' views on architecture. Charles Jencks has described the demolition of the housing project as the death of modern architecture.[5]

As seen from a practicing architect's perspective, Pattern Language was actually an unnatural way of working because the holistic thinking that characterizes good design was thwarted. Also, the method was not as objective as purported. Even the problem formulations actually relied on subjective values. Critics have stated ironically that it was really a case of "value-weighted, value-free choice". Alexander himself has later realized that scientific methods could not help create beautiful buildings and were instead more of a hindrance. Since then, he has renounced his Pattern Language. The dream of a rational design process could not survive the clash with a reality full of conflicting needs and considerations.

Engaging in user-participation in planning, i.e. planning with input from the users, was partly a way for architects to find an objective method as a foundation for planning, in order to have a stronger position in relation to clients, and partly an expression of the desire to defend underprivileged groups. Working to reduce social and economic inequality also provided an opportunity to establish a position in the democracy of the welfare state. This was not an easy task since there were many different categories of experts involved in these politically volatile issues. Generally the question is one of the individual's influence on their own housing and work environment. During this period a new profession has used uncertainties to establish themselves in the building industry—namely project administrators—who are sometimes specialized architects, but more often engineers, taking the position of middlemen between the client, the architect, and the builder.

Scientific methods have, surprisingly, only been of minor help in gauging the user's needs, because knowledge of individual components has not given a direct synthesis or a deeper understanding of the problem. There has been far too little consideration of the fact that specifically in the design process, one change can require another (which Bryan Lawson fittingly compares with a crossword puzzle). On the other hand, the awareness of a general concept of the necessity for a deeper understanding of the user's needs has increased. Nearly always now, during the design and planning of public buildings, focus groups are formed with employees in order to initiate discussion with the designers. In housing construction, the problem of user anonymity has diminished because the rate of building large housing areas has slowed greatly. However, the issue of subjectivity remains.

Humble Assertiveness (an essay)

Design is not a grandiose process. On the contrary, design is mostly a mundane game—or agony. It's a constant balancing act between sensibility on the one hand, and confidence in your own strengths on the other.

The cultural essayist Leif Nylén commented on the annual award of the Casper Salin prize[6] by defining architects as "trend-sensitive master tailors with intellectual ambitions". The word trend-sensitive, or trendy, evokes immediate associations to fashion and superficiality. "The master tailor" is actually a respected craftsman, but, perhaps dependent on different guild traditions or clients, he is considered more subservient than and not as professional as the ironsmith or the carpenter. Finally, the expression "intellectual ambition" instead of "intellectual interests" or "intellectual ability", for example, suggests a discrepancy between pretence and results. If you're inclined to negative interpretations, "architects as trend-sensitive master tailors with intellectual ambitions" is far from flattering. But even so, the description is not totally wrong. As if looking through cracked glass, you can see the connection between sensibility and practical and intellectual work.

Sensibility—the ability to listen, but also the will to absorb impressions—is often associated with sensitivity and artistic disposition. Sensibility is not considered a necessary attribute in jobs that are based on a stable positivist foundation. A civil engineer or an administrator can depend on facts, formulas, and rules in their work. But sensibility is not reserved for artists. A doctor is more likely to find the right diagnosis if he or she does not merely react according to the patient's account of the symptoms, but is also observant of the patient's facial color or eye expressions. Similarly, subtle signs in nature can indicate more to the farmer than the weather forecast.

Notice, however, that the doctor's or the farmer's sensibility need not be all-encompassing. It is focused on certain aspects, the purpose is given, and it is fairly constrained by the occupation itself. That cannot be said of the artist. He or she decides how to use sensibility: extroverted, introverted, or both. The artist also decides freely whether to focus on details, or the entire world. The choice is free—to synthesize feelings or thoughts, big or small.

Sensibility determines what knowledge you are prepared to accept. The sensibility an architect needs to develop has a composite character. It has to be directed toward people, their surroundings, and the relationships between them. All aspects of life are of interest. But to stand between different disciplines and be dependent on them is actually an impossible task.

How can you listen to people that you may never come in contact with? They appear in a variety of groups, represent particular interests, and take different roles. In the end, they still experience architecture with the immediacy of the lone individual.

How can you listen to a plot of land to understand its special character, both in the fragrance of spring and in the chill of an autumn evening?

How do you listen to the soul of a house? How does the baseboard want to meet the lustrous floor? Large and small, light and shadow? How do you listen to the aesthetics?

Knowledge can help, but sensitivity must be applied to encompass so much at one time. You hear and see most clearly, and reach a direct contact with your world, by forgetting your ego (Zen Buddhism comes to mind). To reduce your sense of self by being humble. To identify yourself with the observable, to climb right into the things.

But to formulate an idea and bring it forward in competition with many other possible ideas requires confidence in your own strengths. The pendulum must swing back and forth between humility and self-certainty. Designing rooms and buildings is to swing between chaos and order, between sensibility/humility and belief in your own strengths. And in this process you gradually add to your experience and know-ledge. During education the teacher starts the pendulum swinging and should, ideally, stimulate the search for basic knowledge at the start, but also hone the student's sensibilities and reinforce their self-esteem. Sensibility determines which knowledge and experience they can assimilate. Then, their self-confidence establishes the boundaries for their use. It's not about reaching one pole—of humility or self-certainty—but to continually swing between them. Isn't it true that many architectural failures occur because this pendulum motion has stopped? What is the architect's surrender to building production processes if not a hardened humility? Or is not Le Corbusier's dominance in planning Chandigarh an example of a nearly megalomaniac, rigid self-certainty with no path back to humility? His blind faith in an urban (albeit very aesthetic) vision has destroyed the original local planning principles, and large groups of the population have been excluded. A doctoral thesis on the planning of Chandigarh concludes with these words:

In the conviction that planning practices must remain self-conscious if they are not to become idée's fixes to respond to fast changing realities, this report has attempted to focus attention on several issues in the hope of initiating a lot of rethinking by professional colleagues leading to the emergence of more dynamic practices. (Sahrin 1975, 243)

A non-architect asks: Are there two kinds of architects—the ones who design the beautiful things that get put in the magazines—and the other ones who build the things around us? Answer that if you can! I think that an architect neither hears nor dares anything when the pendulum between humility and self-certainty stops swinging. Uncertainties get camouflaged by an exaggerated belief in other disciplines or in aesthetic role models. When humility no longer reinforces the quality of feelings and thoughts, you only see the surface.

Notes

References

1 Vitruvius in De architectura, or The Ten Books on Architecture, 1st century BC, rediscovered in the 15th century. (1.3.1).

2 Kostof 1977a, 87. According to Kostof, you can therefore see Gothic cathedrals as the manifestation of the doctrine that would arrive hundreds of years later: "form follows function".

3 Sullivan's phrase was wrongly applied by modernists. The word function was Sullivan's expression for metaphysical being (destiny) and not for usage, as it was interpreted by the modernists (Forty 2004, 178).

4 "One should not debate taste."

5 The housing project in San Louis was designed by Minoru Yamasaki (Jencks 1984, 9), the same architect who designed the World Trade Center in Manhattan, which was destroyed on September 11, 2001.

6 The foremost prize in architecture that is awarded in Sweden.

Alberti, Leon Battista: *De Re Aedificatoria 1485*. On the art of building in ten books. MIT Press 1988

Alexander, C; Ishikawa, S; Silverstein, M.: *A Pattern Language. Towns. Buildings. Construction.* Oxford University Press 1977

Anthony, Kathryn H.: *Studio Culture and Student Life. A World of Its Own.* In: Ockman, Joan (ed.): *Architecture School. Three Centuries of Educating Architects in North America.* MIT Press 2012, 396–401

Caldenby, Claes; Walldén, Åsa: *Forskning om arkitektur och gestaltning.* G16: 1986. Statens råd för byggnadsforskning, Stockholm 1986, 6

Colomina, Beatriz with Choi, Esther; Galan, Ignacio G. and Meister, Anna Maria: *Radical Pedagogies in Architectural Education.* Architectural Review, September 28, 2012

Forty, Adrian: *Words and Buildings. A Vocabulary of Modern Architecture.* Thames & Hudson 2004 (2000), 312–314

Gelernter, Mark: *Sources of Architectural Form: A Critical History of Western Design Theory.* Manchester University

Press 1994, 44, 114–115, 239

Jencks, Charles: *The Language of Post-modern Architecture.* Academy Editions, London 1984

Källström, Staffan: *Framtidens katedral.* Stockholm. Carlsson 2000, 190, 205–221

Kostof, Spiro (1977a): *The Architect in the Middle Ages, East and West.* In: Kostof, Spiro (ed.): *The Architect. Chapters in the History of the Profession.* Oxford University Press 1977, 79–80

Kostof, Spiro (1977b): *The Practice of Architecture in the Ancient World: Egypt and Greece.* In: Kostof, Spiro (ed.): *The Architect. Chapters in the History of the Profession.* Oxford University Press 1977, 3–12, 20

Krupinska, Jadwiga: *Om kumulativ forskning och projektering.* Doktorsavhandling. Arkitektursektionen KTH, Stockholm 1983, 74

Lawlor, Robert: *Sacred Geometry. Philosophy and Practice.* Thames & Hudson 1998 (1982)

Lawson, Bryan: *How Designers Think. The Design Process Demystified.* Architectural Press 2008, 60

Linn, Björn: *Från hantverk till funkis.* Byggnadsindustrin nr 17/1966.

MacDonald, William L.: *The Architecture of Roman Empire. An Introductory Study.* Yale University Press 1982, 137–142

Mårtelius, Johan: *Architectus ingenio.* Konsthistorisk tidskrift 2008, Vol. 77, 77–80

Ockman, Joan (ed.): *Architecture School. Three Centuries of Educating Architects in North America.* MIT Press 2012

Olivegren, Johannes: *Brukarplanering. Ett litet samhälle föds: Hur 12 hushåll i Göteborg planerade sitt område och sina hus i kvarteret Klostermuren på Hisingen.* FFFN-s gruppens förlag 1975

Palladio, Andrea: *Fyra böcker om arkitekturen (Quattro libri dell'architettura).* Vinga Bokförlag 1983 (1570)

Rand, Ayn: *The Fountainhead.* Centennial Edition Plume, New York 2005 (1943).

Sarin, Mahdu: *Planning and the Urban Poor. The Chandigarh Experience.* Development Planning Unit, School of Environmental Studies, University College London, December 1975, 243

Simon, Madlen: *Design Pedagogy. Changing Approaches to Teaching Design.* In: Ockman, J. (ed.): *Architecture School. Three Centuries of Educating Architects in North America.* MIT Press 2012, 277

Svedberg, Olle: *Palladio, matematiken och instrumenten.* Konsthistorisk Tidskrift L II/1, 1983

Tschumi, Bernard: *One, Two, Three: Jump.* In: Pearce, Martin; Toy, Maggie (eds): *Educating Architects.* Academy Editions, London 1995, 24–25

Williams, Austin: China. *The progress of an emerging superpower undergoing the largest urbanisation project in human history.* Architectural Review, August 28, 2012

Vitruvius: *Om arkitektur tio böcker.* Byggförlaget, Stockholm 1989 (1.1.1), (1.1.3), (1.2.2)

3 What skills are needed?

You think philosophy is difficult enough, but I tell you it is
nothing to the difficulty of being a good architect.
(Ludwig Wittgenstein 1930)[1]

The difficulty of being a good architect is that, among other things, there can always be several possible solutions to a given problem. Deciding on appropriate priorities can be hard because they must derive from a large, heterogeneous, conflict-ridden (insolvable) field of knowledge. In addition, every priority will have a chain of consequences. Discovering this causes disorientation and uncertainty because you may also not know which tools can be used to control the situation. Knowledge is power according to Western thought but which knowledge is relevant for architects? Can knowledge help cope with subjectivity? Which skills should be prioritized?

What skills are needed—and how can they be taught?

A student from Louisiana State University says:

My undergraduate degree was in biology. I memorized facts
and recited them for tests. Right and wrong answers existed.
Biology labs consisted of experiments that had been conducted
many times before, and the expected outcome was known. The
professors had taught the labs long enough to know what the
students did wrong if the outcome of the experiment produced
unexpected results. (Graham 2003, 2)

Such certainty did not exist at architecture school. It seemed that the teachers did not consider concepts like "right" and "wrong". The historical summary (Chapter 2) shows how the architectural profession, and consequently architectural education, have always hovered in the balance between practical work and theoretical knowledge. What is an architect? An intellectual or a craftsman? In the Swedish Academy Dictionary, an architect is someone with knowledge of the art of building who has the job of drafting plans and drawings for buildings, etc., and who also leads and inspects their construction; a building artist. You can also give a more complete description, for example, that of Architecture Canada RAIC:

> *What is an architect? The most basic definition of an architect*
> *is a professional who is qualified to design and provide advice*
> *—both aesthetic and technical—on built objects in our public*
> *and private landscapes. But this definition barely scratches the*
> *surface of an architect's role. Architects serve as trusted advisors,*
> *their role is holistic, blending diverse requirements and*
> *disciplines in a creative process, while serving the public interest*
> *and addressing health and safety matters. Perhaps, it would*
> *be best to describe architects as conductors who orchestrate*
> *and take the lead in reconciling all the goals for a building*
> *or other structure.*[2]

To be a conductor in that sense, you also have to use artistic imagination and visualization skills, practical and technical knowledge, and social competence, psychological understanding, and ethical insights. To be an architect involves becoming acquainted with all of the proficiencies that Aristotle conceptualized: *epistéme, techne* and *phronesis*. *Epistéme* is scientific knowledge, independent of context, unchanging over time. *Techne* are the practical empirical skills of handcraft and they also include artistic and technical skills. These evolve together with societal development and can be attained through applied practice. *Phronesis* is to know which action is correct in a specific situation. This cannot be obtained through training, but is instead developed by being part of a culture or a profession. *Phronesis* is the kind of wisdom we can never forget once learned. The architect's dual roles of artist and technician can be hard to unify:

*As "artist", the architect is seen as a giver of forms, constrained—
perhaps unhappily—by the demands and the limited resources
of his client or patron. As a functional specialist, the architect is
seen as bringing his design competence and special knowledge
to the fulfillment of individual and social needs. In the world
of contemporary architectural practice and education, the two
views of the profession tend to polarize, each view suggesting
a very different answer to the questions posed by the shifts in
architectural practice.* (Schön 1985, 3)

About two thousand years ago, Vitruvius wrote that architects have
to consider *firmitas, utilitas and venustas,* in other words, *durability,
utility and beauty.* This demanded a comprehensive education. An
architect should be:

*skilful with the pencil, instructed in geometry, know
much history, have followed the philosophers with attention,
understand music, have some knowledge of medicine, know
the opinions of the jurists, and be acquainted with astronomy
and the theory of the heavens.* (Vitruvius 1.1.3)

Vitruvius realized that an architect needed basic theoretical knowledge in these fields; not even specialists could attain perfection. But
an architect must be "*both naturally gifted and amenable to instruction*".

Today the necessary skills for the architectural profession are not
very different from the time of Vitruvius, but the terminology has
changed. *Durability* is now related to structural engineering, building physics and building construction, plus building materials,
which includes their durability, aging, environmental aspects and
possible recycling. *Utility* has to do with functionality and the
specifics of different uses, but is perhaps more a question of psychology and ergonomics, human dimensions, physiological and cultural
needs and habits, both individually and in groups. The word *beauty*
sounds obsolete in terms of buildings. Today we prefer to say interesting form or good design, perhaps because these words seem

more concrete and easier to combine with rational terms that make the world more understandable. You can hardly say that about the word "*beauty*", which is immediately interpreted to be loaded with subjectivity. But values and aesthetic preferences, shaped over many years in our culture, are the foundation for any judgment, not just the aesthetic ones. *So what is new? Nothing much. Our problems are as they were in Roman times*" says the leading English architectural theoretician Geoffrey Broadbent.

Vitruvius' text from around 15 BC, rediscovered in the early Renaissance, and later Alberti's text, from the 1400s, created a framework for how the theoretical discussion about architectural education was carried forward. Vitruvius' comprehensive list of subjects that architects should be familiar with placed the architect *inside* an expansive field of knowledge, meaning architects should study other disciplines as well as architecture. In contrast, Alberti was considerably more focused on the architectural discipline as such and on its limited interdisciplinary needs.

Frank Weiner, who got first prize for his essay on how "new knowledge" could influence architectural education writes:[3]

> *Vitruvius' formulation has to do with the relationship of an architect to the idea of an educated life, whereas Alberti's formulation is about the relationship of life to the idea of a professionally educated architect. There is a positive tension between these two fundamental positions, and perhaps a good school of architecture should strive for reciprocity between the Vitruvian and the Albertian approaches to architectural education.* (Weiner 2005, 21)

It is hard to comprehensively cover the architect's field of knowledge during the five years of education that is common in many countries. Therefore, the architect's role in relationship to the needs of society determines the priorities. Different subjects are introduced and the focus and field of study contribute to the profile of each school. To expand one subject encroaches on the other subjects or the available studio time. A survey of students at Swedish design and architectural schools shows that balancing these needs is difficult. While architecture students felt they had good design education, but too few academic subjects, landscape architecture students said the opposite. They complained that they had too many academic subjects and too little time for design work in their projects. Establishing a curriculum is like a balancing act which requires the ability to set proper limits for the different subjects and also to give the teachers room for creative interpretations. The curriculum can be so extensive that students hardly have time to reflect on what they have learned. Students may register the knowledge, but they may only be conscious of it later on in their studies or during practical work after their education. The maturing process is individual.

According to Professor Björn Linn, to satisfy the architect's professional need for knowledge, at least five different models for architectural education have been used:

The Apprentice Model—the traditional English model. This involved practical training in an architectural firm. It included drafting skills and actual contact with construction projects, but was probably deficient in theoretical education.

The Academic Model (introduced at the École Royale des Beaux Arts) had a strong emphasis on drawing skills, but also on art and theo-retical education. As time went on, it was considered somewhat formalistic and rigid.

The Technical University Model, with its roots in Germany, was based on a solid foundation in building technology and general technology with the addition of craft training.

The Bauhaus Model was an education that started with extensive material studies, together with arts and crafts, later coalescing into architectural design.

The Bartlett Model. A British model from the 1960s which separated "*analysis*" from "*synthesis*", *but with undeveloped logic.* It was based on project work in order to forge a connection with the real world, but in fact, skills were lost and planning was difficult.

At present, architectural education in design institutes around the world—in other words, schools that educate architects, interior architects, landscape architects and industrial designers—contains a combination of three study traditions with different pedagogical methods:

1 scientific knowledge within the humanities and technology (*why?*)
2 craft and artistic training as skills (*how?*)
3 design work—creative studio projects with the application of knowledge from humanities and technology, plus art and craft skills (*what?*)

I will give a short description later of the subjects and skills that fall within these learning traditions. I will also cover the different aspects of language in architectural education in a special section, see p. 78.

Additionally, in several countries there are different types of post graduate education that include the architect's role in leadership and professionalism, problems in society where architecture and urban planning are central, planning regulations, building restoration, etc. Architectural schools are rarely independent institutions like the Oslo School of Architecture and Design (AHO), but are rather part of other institutions. They can be part of a technical institute, as in Stockholm, a university, as in Umeå, or an art academy, as in Copenhagen. These different associations illustrate the difficulty of placing architecture within one discipline such as engineering, humanities or art. Even if the fundamental teaching methods are the same, specific subjects and aspects can be emphasized in different ways. The renowned private school of architecture, The Architectural Association School of Architecture (AA) in London, has a special position because it was established in the middle of the 1800s with the intent to radically change architectural education.

Independence and separation from the state are the hallmark of the school, which does not have a formal curriculum. Students choose a studio within which they can create their own course plans.

*Subjective originality and empathy for the full performance of archi-
tecture, physically and poetically, shape their programmes* (Balfour
1995, 78). Several internationally known architects studied at AA.

Scientific factual knowledge

Within most other disciplines at higher education level, teaching
methods are used which are designed to gradually impart further
knowledge in well-defined, sometimes very specific areas of study.
In technical subjects, the emphasis is on abstract formulas and calculations, while in the humanities, theories and critical examination
of references and sources are fundamental. The student's knowledge
is evaluated through examinations.

The wide scope of the architectural discipline necessitates a different
type of teaching. The big challenge in formulating a curriculum is in
delineating the required subjects to give a good orientation and the
necessary understanding, without getting lost in specialist studies.
The key is to secure knowledge; to learn terms, facts, rules of thumb,
and with those, to build up a reference and knowledge base so that
the student can, if necessary, seek deeper proficiency by themselves.
Sooner or later, the student discovers that an architectural career
requires lifelong learning.

> *Neither the questions nor answers exist before the situation
> arises. The architect can provide a shortcut. By sketching, he or
> she can build a model of the situation that illustrates at least
> some aspects of it and makes it possible to make a preliminary
> assessment. Experience and knowledge improve the ability to
> assess situations.* (Linn 1982, 4)

In the years after 1968, design teaching was weakened, while social
studies like sociology and ethnology were strengthened. In addition,
belief in the superiority of rational thought increased to the point
that architectural education as a whole began to have an identity cri-
sis. Concurrently, a greater interest arose for architectural history,

urban renewal and historical renovation. A recovery at the Swedish schools followed more the Vitruvian rather than Albertian teaching model. In the 1980s there was a stronger interest in architectural history; in the 1990s in philosophy, especially phenomenology and hermeneutics, and currently there is a strong interest in climate change and environmental issues with a focus on sustainability, and landscape studies. This generates an interest in building materials, building construction and building physics, combined with the possibilities created by digital techniques. Many of the objectives that were once thought to be very important have been de-emphasized.

These swings in focus have been commented on by architect Rem Koolhaas, a previous student at AA, in the book *Conversations with Students*. He says that schools are part of the same culture around the world; steered by a collective subconscious. During some periods there are architectural aspects that are very important while other things are ignored. Then, those subjects that were very important become forgotten and the ones that were ignored are given greater emphasis. Distinct ideas only surface when strong individuals wield their dictatorial power.

Scientifically based humanistic subjects

Architects take their proposals into the interface between past and future within a context of existing buildings and traditions. The passing down of knowledge and experience from one generation to another is central to architecture. *Architectural history* has always nourished contemporary architectural debate. Swedish courses in architectural history focus on Swedish, Western and non-European architecture and urban planning and their relationship to society: world views and ideation. The studies include the foundations of architecture, basic theories, and concepts in a cultural and historical perspective from antiquity to the present day. In principle, the subject is taught by applying well-established traditional knowledge of cultural history, but often with supplemental exercises that reinforce the learning in various ways. For example, developing drawings of an ancient Greek temple, from given fragments of building parts, illustrates the ancient concept of beauty and its sensual meaning. Cultural traditions can be brought to life when you see them through the lens of specific color schemes for buildings in different parts of the world, from different eras.

One subject that has a special status because of its focus on the foundations of design has various titles in different countries: *Basic Design, Theoretical and Applied Aesthetics or Architectural Forms.* Sometimes this is integrated within studio work instead of being treated as a separate subject. At any rate, this involves skills and knowledge that are of great importance in developing an architectonic awareness. This field of study encompasses basic architectural design and the nature of architectural space, form, and materials. The direction of the courses can be theoretical as well as practical with large doses of a phenomenological perspective. Basic concepts of how we experience space, like *the play of mass and void, physical and virtual boundaries, color, light, and tactility*, are presented in lectures and exercises. In these exercises, subjective interpretations are encouraged so that the student can be receptive to emotions and experiences in the creative process. The subject must therefore touch on art, descriptive geometry, perception psychology, etc., and it lays the foundation for thinking in architectonic terms.

Architectural theory is a general concept for thoughts on architecture, tirelessly but not systematically built through millennia. Theories about architecture are inherently vague because they attempt to establish concepts in a world that is mostly visual and highly subjective. The questions that emerge often concern the ethics and aesthetics of architecture. The importance of prioritizing ethical aspects over the aesthetic and visual is often stressed. Architectural theory relies on knowledge of architectural history but it does not have the same academic rigor. Sometimes it can seem more like an ideology or viewpoint that indicates a direction, rather than a theory than can explain something, and many times it can simply be opinions that give a deeper understanding of architecture. This applies to the texts of Vitruvius and Alberti, as well as to those of contemporary practicing architects Peter Zumthor, Juhani Pallasmaa and Steven Holl. Even texts on gender studies fit this description. These texts often introduce viewpoints that help people understand paradigm shifts in society. The foremost service of architectural theory is to give a broader view of architectural practice. An example of this is *Built upon Love: Architectural Longing after Ethics and Aesthetics*, a book that has been written by the phenomenologically oriented architectural theorist Pérez-Gómez, in which he tries to show a deep connection between the ethical and poetic values of architecture by stating that *"Ethics and aesthetics reduced to rules are useless: ethical action is always singular and circumstantial. It always seems miraculous and unique"* (Pérez-Gómez 2006, 4).

The development of architectural theory as a subject in architectural education has evolved from the "theoretical practice" that was established, according to Bernard Tschumi, during the third stage of separation between architecture and construction after 1968 (see Chapter 2). It is interesting to look more closely at architectural theory as a subject in the light of the earlier description of the split be-tween architecture and construction.

Theory and practice in the contemporary discourse

Many theorists, most often connected to the academic world, stress the need to study architectural theory. Neil Leach says that schools of architecture should stop limiting themselves to architectural projects. Courses on groundbreaking philosophers' texts should instead establish a critical relationship with the architectural profession and give a better understanding of society. This view is not without controversy. For example, the phenomenologically-based architectural theorist, Juhani Pallasmaa, states the opposite; that today's tendency to theorize robs architecture of its materiality.

The current over-emphasis on the intellectual and conceptual dimensions of architecture further contributes to the disappearance of the physical, sensual and embodied essence of architecture.… Instead of being an embodied existential metaphor conveyed through the tectonic materiality of building, architecture is seen to derive and communicate its meaning through networks of discourse. There is a curious air of both over-intellectualization and mystification, of opening and closing, revealing and hiding. Much of today's theorizing seems to be a matter of taking distance from the reality of architecture more than attempting to understand its essence. (Pallasmaa 2005, 66)

Plato's idea that the conceptual world is superior to the world that we experience via our senses has had too great an influence on the Western way of prioritizing knowledge. But according to Geoffrey Broadbent (1995), an architect cannot work on a "pure thinking" level or ignore the world of the senses, because everything he or she does will affect the senses of everyone who uses those buildings and environments. If architectural education is over-intellectualized, and if feelings and sensuality are not part of the process, it can produce "eyes that don't see".

That trend-sensitive architects use the new theories of philosophers and sociologists in their argumentation (perhaps unnecessarily) for their own ideas is often met with criticism from other disciplines. The American philosopher Roger Scruton (1979) points out that doctrines in architectural theory are highly erratic; sometimes they touch on the nature of architecture, sometimes its values and criteria, and sometimes how we experience it. There are also faulty interpretations. He states, for example, that one of the favorite concepts of Modernism, *Time and Space*, is based on a misconception, because the dimension of time is seen as equivalent to the three spatial dimensions. Scruton criticizes several elements in the foundation of architectural theory, perhaps because he wants to apply the rules of philosophy to something that does not claim to be a philosophical discipline. He says himself that in the field of philosophy, theoretical knowledge is in pursuit of the truth. On the other hand, the practical knowledge that the architect needs is based on activities and emotions, and it requires a substitute for the truth.

However, architects are hardly as naive as Scruton would like us to believe. Despite its collective name, architectural theory has generally been in pursuit of this substitute truth, even while dreaming about eternal truths. But the path toward realizing these dreams has often been tortuous. The architects of the Renaissance made mistakes when interpreting the traditions of the ancients, but that didn't prevent them from creating impressive works of architecture. Le Corbusier lacked skills in mathematics, and according to architectural theorist and practitioner Johan Linton, he made errors in the construction of his famous measuring system, the Modulor, which is based on the Golden Ratio. And when Peter Eisenman was told that he had misinterpreted linguistic theorist Noam Chomsky's syntax theories,[4] he admitted directly that for him it wasn't a matter of understanding theories. He used them as *inspiration* for architectonic design, which was what he wanted to be renowned for.[5]

There are many examples of theories and input from different disciplines being used by architects as inspiration in artistic interpretations, and occasionally as "*scientific camouflage*". The American philosophy professor John Silber is annoyed by Daniel Libeskind's verbal descriptions of the buildings he has designed. Silber says disdainfully that it is "theory-speak"—an unnecessary, pretentious and misleading shell.

Architecture is not easily represented in theoretical explanations, says Alberto Pérez-Gómez.

*While theory of architecture may be rooted in mythic or poetic
stories, philosophy, theology, or scientia during different times
of its history, architecture is none of these but an event;
it is ephemeral, yet it has the power to change one's life in
the present, like magic or an erotic encounter.*
(Pérez-Gómez 2006, 109)

Insight into different disciplines can contribute to the architect's general education, but what started as a struggle to break free from the power of the guilds several hundred years ago by introducing academic study should not be pushed too far. The units of architectural theory that are presented during a student's time at architectural school have to alternate between distance and nearness to professional practice in order to teach the flexibility and awareness that is needed in the architect's way of thinking, without losing the profession's unique quality. The humanistic subjects affect the value systems and contribute needed references to the development of the architect's vocabulary of concepts.

Technical subjects

The existence or scope of technical subjects in architectural education can vary depending on the organization that the architectural school belongs to and also on the tradition that guides it.

The basic technical skills that architects need in their work can be summarized by the Vitruvian concept of *firmitas,* i.e. durability. The main subjects in this group are building statics, building physics and the study of materials. *Building statics* deals with the product's, i.e. the building's or site work's, equilibrium while being exposed to different forces, for example, increased loading or wind. The main focus is on the building's structure and its function: maximum spans for beams and floor slabs, sizing of load-bearing components like walls and columns at different loads, etc.

In other words, the idea is to find out how far you can go before a construction fails, and which constructions are optimal (including economically). The limits of building statics determine how far you can twist a construction, for example, Turning Torso in Malmö by Santiago Calatrava, or the maximum allowable cantilever for a console construction. Studying the kinetics of the human body can also help to understand the fundamentals of statics. Santiago Calatrava used this technique when he studied and drew his hand movements as a basis for his sketches of the advanced, sinuous canopies (shaped like a cupped hand) over the railway platforms in Zürich.

In contrast, *building physics* focuses mostly on protection from climate effects, directly comparable to the role that clothing plays for humans: protection against rain, wind and cold for the head, the feet, and the entire body, in the same way you want to avoid leaks and drafts through roofs and walls, as well as moisture and water transfer into a building's basement or foundation. Both building statics and building physics have to be closely integrated with the study of *building materials* because different materials can have entirely different qualities in terms of load bearing and climate protection.

For engineers, the study of technical subjects involves calculating the dimensions of structural components, as, for example, the thickness of a bridge column or a load-bearing wall, the required insulation thickness, etc. For architects, the corresponding studies do not necessarily include such calculations, but instead the student is encouraged to develop a professional judgment and an understanding for *reasonable approximations* that apply in different situations. Teachers in technical subjects must have a special ability to educate architects. The proper starting point for developing judgment in material studies can be Louis Kahn's question to a material: *What do you want to be?* What does the brick want to be? The metal sheet? While bricks want to be laid up as a wall or arch, the same does not apply to materials that are cast or stamped.

The Italian engineer Pier Luigi Nervi became interested in his work in visible and invisible relationships between the technical and aesthetic aspects of buildings. His renowned engineering skills led to him being named Professor of Poetry (!) at Harvard University in 1961. In his lectures, he touched on the differences between teaching architects versus engineers:

> *The substantial difference between teaching statics to architects and to engineers lies in the fact that architects must possess such an understanding and mastery of the static–constructional field*

The residential tower Turning Torso in Malmö, Sweden, designed
by Santiago Calatrava, was completed in 2005. The 54-storey
structure is based on nine twisting muscular forms, each with
five apartment stories. Photo: Sture Samuelsson

Palazzetto dello Sport, 1957, Piazza Apollodoro, Rome, Italy, built
for the 1960 Summer Olympic Games. Thanks to an extensive use
of prefab concrete modules, the dome was erected in only 40 days.
Design: Pier Luigi Nervi. Photo: Jadwiga Krupinska

as to be able to create and approximately dimension new struc-
tural-architectural solutions, while it is sufficient for engineers
to have such a knowledge of mathematical theories as to enable
them to analyze and dimension exactly the various parts of an
already defined structure. (Nervi 1965, 191)

Technical instruction for architects works best when it alternates between theory with examples, and direct applications, or from experiments to theory. The Danish professor Erik Reitzel[6] intro-duced this kind of exercise in statics. The assignment also included a playful competition between the students, which reinforced their learning. The goal was to use practical experiments to grasp funda-mental theoretical formulas in statics. Students built bridges with a few sheets of paper and then tried to load them with as many bricks as possible. The data from the failures of the structures was summarized and used to illustrate formulas for the relationship be-tween loads and the length of spans. This aided the students' ability to make approximations. They got a feel for reasonable conditions, rather than exact calculations. That is exactly what an architect needs—to be able to work with details while being aware of the entirety, and in reverse, to be aware of the details while working on the whole.

A Few Words About Concrete (A short lecture)

Who hasn't noticed that white wine isn't white at all, but instead, slightly yellowish (but still good)? And "flip-flopping" in politics doesn't mean that you actually do a somersault. Perhaps the prefix "concrete" in the Swedish term for the maligned "concrete suburbs" does not mean that they are always miserable.

The word "concrete" lives a dual life. In one life, it is a powerful word that brings drama to every story. If you say concrete colossus, concrete grey, or strong as concrete, the colossus is impenetrable, the grey is deeper than imaginable, and the strength is irresistible. In the other life, (reinforced) concrete is what we build with—"the most agreeable and exquisite construction process ever invented by man"—as Pier Luigi Nervi put it 50 years ago. It is quite possible that he would say the same thing today.

In any event, you must see that modern architecture, both conceptual and realized, has sprung from the possibilities of reinforced concrete. Le Corbusier's five points of modern architecture were in fact a description of what concrete is capable of. Interestingly, 30 years earlier, around 1900, the talented entrepreneur François Hennebique wanted to achieve the same things for his own home: large cantilevers, consoles; a roof garden. Hennebique provided several innovations and his contribution to the development of reinforced concrete was enormous. To have the right to be called a "Hennebique entrepreneur" was very prestigious at the turn of the 20th century. However, the style that he used for his show house was more a kind of Gothic with Oriental overtones. It was not modern architecture.

The magnificent construction over the entry ramp to Il Lingotto—the Fiat factory in Torino, designed by Giacomo Mattè Trucco—can be considered a successful reply to Guarino Guerini's Baroque cupola in the same city. August Perret, who incidentally became an honorary member of the Swedish Academy in 1930, said that "the most appropriate use of a new material will always create a new style". He had himself laid part of the groundwork for the new style, but the big

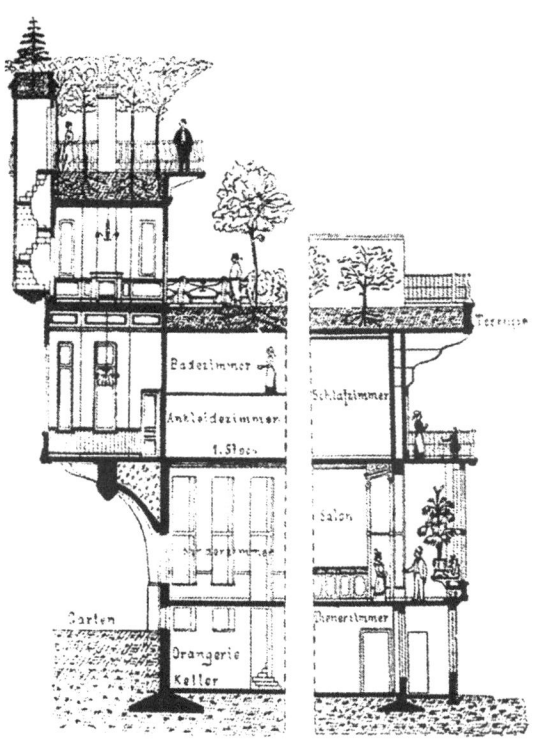

One of the pioneers of reinforced concrete, François Hennebique,
designed his own house in Bourg-la-Reine, France, in 1904.
The cantilever (daring for the time), the roof garden, and several
innovative construction details were made possible by reinforced
concrete, but the design was traditional.
Archive, The School of Architecture KTH

Left: The entrance to a car test track on the roof of the Il Lingotto Fiat factory in Torino, Italy, designed by Giacomo Mattè Trucco, 1915–1921. Photo: Jadwiga Krupinska

Right: It is possible that Giacomo Mattè Trucco got his inspiration for the spectacular concrete roof over the ramp to the test track from Guarino Guerini´s dome in the Baroque Sindone Chapel, which is also in Torino. Photo: Robin Evans © MIT

breakthrough occurred together with Le Corbusier's five points of modern architecture, namely:

1) the house on pilotis, or reinforced concrete stilts
2) the free facade
3) the open floor plan
4) ribbon windows
5) a roof garden

These five points, that have influenced architecture around the world for decades, should actually be seen as the artistic summary of the answer to the query: what can concrete do? It is a summary done with an architect's sensitivity to his time and it shows his interest in the capabilities of the material (to drive this point home, he even used these principles for the guard house at Villa Savoye). Here you find a respect for the material qualities of concrete, recognized as its embodied sensibility and substantiality; an ethical, aesthetic dimension. At any rate, this generated a design language like nothing before. Historical references lost their value. Only the future (bearing with it, concrete) had any interest. Modern architecture became more or less synonymous with concrete, and they strode forth together into the heroic period of Modernism.

Perhaps nowadays you don't see concrete as something heroic, but it evolves steadily to meet new demands. A whole family of different concrete materials and products exceed at formability, strength, thermal storage, sound and thermal insulation, fire protection, moisture resistance, etc., and with the aid of new methods, work processes have been simplified.

It's interesting to take a look around and think about what today's architecture is saying to us. Professor Hal Foster from Princeton University talks about two trends in today's designs.[7] One is "spectacular architecture" in the wake of Frank Gehry's Guggenheim in Bilbao. The other trend is "trauma architecture" exemplified by Daniel Libeskind's architecture, including his designs for the World Trade Center or the Jewish Museum in Berlin. Of course there are many other possible

The school in Paspels, Switzerland (1998) is beautifully adapted
to the slope and has solid concrete walls that form the framework
of the building. In contrast, the classrooms are clad completely
in timber, creating a warm and intimate atmosphere.
Architect: Valerio Olgiati. Photo: Heinrich Helfenstein

perspectives; we can all try our own. Realizing that it's difficult to see your own time, I can still discern some clear trends in contemporary architecture by looking at building materials:
 - Testing boundaries
 (weight and mass; the immaterial—transparence)
 - Minimalism, but also artificial landscapes and nature

In all of these directions, concrete can be relevant in different ways. Testing limits has always been the role of concrete, which actually has not always been without drama. A series of concrete failures as late as the 1950s in the USA were caused by a lack of understanding for how concrete works; what it wants. But they have learned from their mistakes. In concert with steel, concrete can resist gravity and structural forces. The threatening, leaning structures bring forth strong emotions; moments of terror. Will they stay up? And then we feel relieved because we trust concrete to hold, despite its weight and mass (or thanks to it).

It's hard for concrete to be relevant in the field of transparency; or striving to be immaterial. But through its presence it does emphasize the fragility of adjacent materials. Also, who knows what will happen in the future? There have been successful tests making translucent concrete, achieving good strength by using optical fibers as fine aggregate.

Within minimalism (which you could call a new edition of modernism), many very beautiful and interesting buildings have been built with concrete. Here the raw, often polished or sometimes pigmented concrete is a vital part of the sensory experience. While the previous direction used ambiguous boundaries, this involves a kind of sensuous precision.

Between these two polar opposites—the massive, heavy, threatening and the immaterial, disappearing—there is architecture that wants to be friendly, like nature or (artificial) landscapes. Concrete can then be sensual as in the work of the Spanish architect and pioneer Miguel Fisac or in the swelling art museum addition by Zaha Hadid, shaped of self-compacted concrete with the sensation of smooth, dark skin.[8]

Left: The extension of the Ordrupgaard Museum in Copenhagen, Denmark, in 2005, seeks to establish a new landscape, but at the same time to create new relations with the existing conditions. Architect: Zaha Hadid. Photo: © Roland Halbe Architekturfotografie

Right: A conceptual sketch by Zaha Hadid to the extension of the Ordrupgaard Museum. Photo: Zaha Hadid Architects

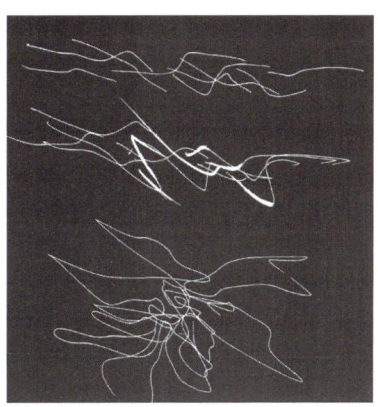

The extension of Ordrupgaard Museum, 2005. Interior of the cafeteria. Architect: Zaha Hadid. Photo: © Helen Binet

Concrete gives the architect many opportunities to work with sensual expression, as long as you ask it what it can and what it wants, and you search for the answers as an architect would interpret it. Then, perhaps, the prefix concrete can start appearing in new combinations: concrete malleable, concrete economical, concrete strong, concrete beautiful.

Arts, crafts, and skills (practical knowledge)

Historically, handcrafts have held a special position in architectural education—as the cradle of the profession. This was revived emphatically in the Bauhaus, where students undertook a thorough foundation in crafts before they joined courses in architecture. Practical work in the studios with the design and production of objects in wood, metal, textiles, paint, glass, plaster and stone was supplemented with theoretical work, including nature studies, structures, geometry, color and composition, plus presentation, materials, and tools. Renowned artists who were enlisted as teachers were given great liberty to influence the students' values, which, in Johannes Itten's case involved mysticism, which was later severely criticized. Geoffrey Broadbent calls the Bauhaus teaching system a mish-mash of theoretical and craft education. Considering the strong influence that Bauhaus design has had on design, in architecture, industrial and graphic design, etc., this mish-mash must have been clearly well mixed to nourish an artistic and innovative way of thinking. This coincided, incidentally, with the needs of industries that were hungry for product designs that could be put into mass production.

The combination of art and craft has long been the hallmark of the Danish system of architectural education. The Royal Danish Academy of Fine Arts, School of Architecture (KADK) was founded in the middle of the 18th century to train artists, and a few decades later it was supplemented with training for craftsmen. Most of the applicants who wanted to become architects had done some kind of four-year craft training before entering their architecture studies. This may have been somewhat detrimental to the general education for architects, since a scholastic degree was not a prerequisite. In some cases, the notable pragmatic position could reduce interest in more abstract, imaginative thinking, but in return, the architects, with their practical knowledge of crafts, could be employed by clients as competent advisors to supervise construction. This contributed to the well-known high quality of Danish architecture and building (for a current example, see the photo on p. 83).

Even until the end of the 1990s, there was still the opportunity to have a craft education equated with a high school education in order to get into architectural school at university level. This possibility was removed when the European Union brought about a restructuring of higher education in Europe. However, the older Danish architects who had trained as masons or carpenters and had a practical knowledge and a sensual relationship with materials still influence Danish building tradition and furniture design.

The judgment of the architect can be refined by practical training—periods of craft and trainee work on the construction site. To a certain extent, this mandatory training has replaced the craft subjects at different architectural schools. The chance to forge a deeper understanding of materials and tools during trainee work gradually declined as the construction industry made the transition from handcrafts to factory production of building components and to an industrial assembly process for large projects. Within the smaller construction projects there were fewer resources for mentoring trainees. On the other hand, various elective handcraft courses have been offered to increase the awareness of different building materials and their characteristics. For the past two decades at the Royal Institute of Technology School of Architecture in Stockholm, there have been many practical courses for students using wood, concrete and plaster, where students design and build, for example, street and park furniture. Unfortunately, many of these courses have fallen by the wayside when coursework has been replaced by studio projects. The practical courses have been dependent on the initiative of

Examples of street furniture designed and built in a factory by students participating in an elective summer course, in cooperation with Swedish concrete producers. Photo: Carolina Krupinska

enthusiastic teachers, not on the established curriculum.

Practicing life drawing, painting still life or sculpting gives an opportunity to develop sensibility, sensitivity for form and material awareness, among other things. When you concentrate on sensory impressions and think about color, light and shadow, space, surface, the lightness and the mass of an entity, you also change the rhythm and character of your thought process. In design work, the intellect is highly involved and thoughts are introverted, targeting inner visions. In artistic work, the emotions are fully engaged and your attention is directed outward—to see (with new vision). Alternating between the intellectual and the artistic helps establish the flexibility that every architect needs in their work.

A training in arts and practical skills is a way of giving students the analog and digital tools they need to actualize their thoughts in the form of sketches, illustrations, drawings and models. These tools are of utmost importance in the most characteristic aspect of the profession, namely the act of sketching, which will be covered in detail in Chapter 5. Different techniques may be used for sketching: pencil or ink drawing, watercolor, physical or digital models, occasionally mock-ups, and more rarely, verbal formulations, etc. Any sketch is steered by the tool that is used. The key is to search for your own form of expression and find a sketching technique that helps you retrieve creative images from your subconscious. The practice of these techniques is essential.

Language and drawings

The majority of students starting at architectural school have a very vague idea of what the profession involves and how the teaching is done. Many new words pop up that are hard to understand, like *spatial sequences, interstitial space, voids, grids,* and *clusters.* It's very difficult to grasp their meanings. But architecture can be explained in pretentious, pompous or common-sense ways. Everyday language or formulations from novels can often replace professional terms, making the relationship to what you are drawing less abstract. For example, we offered a studio project involving scenography and the design of a mobile stage, followed by two months of designing a theater. The idea with the scenography course was to introduce new dimensions and a deeper understanding for the word "functional", which is often tossed around casually. Instead of function, this was about dramatic events in surroundings that had to produce involvement and compassion. It was also very evident how important material expression is in creating a specific atmosphere.

The literary critic Thomas Anderberg says that reading is *letting a world take shape inside us, a world that will be molded in different ways by different readers* (2009, 148). Literary texts are important for architects, because just like other types of artistic expression, words can help them form perceptions about life and create imaginary worlds when he or she "molds" shapes and spaces into human surroundings.

Opinions on the meaning of language in architecture have changed over time. Professor of Architecture Adrian Forty reminds us that, for example, during Modernism, Mies van der Rohe´s famous admonition *Build—don't talk* was so prevalent that serious investigations of the relationship and interdependence between architecture and language were effectively forbidden. Such a standpoint is in stark contrast to the previously described relationship to language during the third split between architecture and construction (Chapter 2), when the concept of *theoretical practice* was established and many young architects chose to write about and publish their works in lieu of building them.

Even the meaning of words can change over time. For example, the concept of *movement* had a deeply symbolic meaning during Modernism as an expression of a faith in the future and in the dynamism of society. The introduction of new building materials like reinforced concrete and expansive glass liberated architecture from the constraints of walls. You could break away from the old "static"

Arne Jacobsen's isometric perspective of the House of the Future
—designed together with Flemming Lassen and built for a Danish
housing exhibition in 1929. The dynamism of the building, based
on a composition of circles and spirals, is strengthened by that era's
dreams of cars, boats and helicopters. Danish National Art Library

architecture and its symmetrically organized plans. To really experience expanding space, the penetration of outside space with inside and vice versa, you had to move through it. *Movement* (always forward) illustrated the aim of modernist architecture to be seen as progressive and literally—modern. Almost without exception, architectural drawings from this era contain images of helicopters, steamships or cars in movement. It is interesting to note that the concept of *movement* does not have the same connection to a belief in the future anymore. The word is now interpreted prosaically, and has been objectified, in that it just helps to describe flows and functions, explain processes, and quantify spaces and transport.

During the discussions in the 1970s about user-planning, the importance of language in the communication between different participating groups came under scrutiny. The introduction of the terms *soft data* and *hard data* illustrated the relationship between objectivity and subjectivity in communication with users, as well as with separate consultants. Hard data that may be expressed in terms of numbers, areas, standard specifications, etc. was (and still is) the "expert's" powerful argument because it is presented as figures that speak for themselves. It is readily accepted in planning situations, but can actually be a way of camouflaging the subjectivity and uncertainty that always exists in the building process. Soft data is based on professional, tacit knowledge, expresses cultural aspects, values and ethical/aesthetical aspects, and may be construed as unclear. Bureaucrats and client "representatives" prefer hard data, probably because it is easier to gather, while applying soft data requires a holistic grasp of the situation and a belief in one's own human experience.

Adrian Forty discusses drawings and language as two different ways to present architectonic ideas. He feels that it is not completely uncontroversial that drawings are always considered superior to words. You have to realize that just as drawings have different qualities, and gradually evolve from the ambiguity of the sketch to the exactitude of the construction drawing, so does language.

An experienced architect can quickly get an overview of an architectural project by studying drawings and pictures. Getting the same insight by listening or reading is much harder, takes more time, and is perhaps not always worth the effort.

Drawings, models and visual representations form a new language that students absorb during their studies. Words are needed as a supplement to better understand their own thoughts, doubts and subconscious choices that are mainly based on unspoken, tacit knowledge. Drawings give an immediate overview of an idea, while words are spoken or written in accordance with given rules in a linear fashion to add emotion and describe feelings. Successive sequences of movement can therefore be better represented by language than with drawings. Describing the feeling of just stepping in and "wandering around" in an entirely imaginary building makes the project less abstract. You can easily apply Professor Erik Lundberg's description of occupying a space, any space that we enter, and simultaneously processing an assortment of sensations: where is the center, where are the boundaries? In our thoughts we can touch the walls, move around the room and experience it as space. In the same way, you can occupy spaces that do not yet exist and give them substance.

Language can help me verbalize for myself and others what I see, hear, what I can smell, what I like or dislike when I "step into" an imaginary building or environment. Both sensual and functional aspects can be illustrated and realized. Describing an out-of-body experience in a projected, as yet un-embodied environment articulates one's own subjectivity.

A verbal description can also more easily convey material and spatial aspects which are not captured well in drawings. Such a subjective portrayal appeals to our emotions. Language frees the mind. Special architectural terms are not needed for this, just an ability to imagine places not yet real, and to communicate them to other people. The precise nature of poetry can be a guide. An entirely different choice of words may be needed when interpreting a certain

"8HOUSE" ("8TALLET")—multi-family housing in Ørestad,
Copenhagen, completed 2009–2012. Arkitekt BIG—Bjarke Ingels
Group. Photo: Jadwiga Krupinska

problem or while explaining its functional or technical aspects. Language may be used to express ethical standpoints which support the existence of architecture and its cultural legacy.

Bernard Tschumi makes a distinction between the concepts of *buildings* and *architecture*. *Buildings* can be constructed without drawings, while *architecture* does not exist without drawings, just as it does not exist without words, since architecture involves much more than the building process. It embodies and expresses cultural, social and philosophical strata that have developed gradually through the centuries. Architecture may be seen as a kind of knowledge that, just like other types of knowledge, can be expressed in different ways. In the architectural discourse, words can be as important as buildings (Tschumi 1980, 152).

But what does *architecture* contribute to *buildings*? Professor Bill Hillier attempts to give an answer: architecture, in contrast to buildings, consists of the conscious intellectual choices that the architect makes throughout the process of creative work. The space and form—their possibilities and their limits—are the raw potential.

However, of course, as in all other professions, architecture does have a professional language. As an example, names of different architects are used frequently, which may seem to be cryptic "name-dropping" to the unacquainted, but this is actually a way of summarizing complex situations and ways to think and create. It may be described as a specific variety of the shorthand of the stenographer. Names represent both symbols and sentences that summarize characteristic methods for solving certain problems, historically as well as today. Saying "Mies van der Rohe" unlocks an array of modernist thoughts and design language: distinct lines, meticulous treatment of materials, colors, details, and an ascetic style in line with his mantra: *less is more*. Something entirely different comes to mind when you mention Bofill's design vocabulary, which is immediately associated with a pompous expression, but with a fairly plain use of materials. Introducing references like these not only increases our awareness of our place in the stream of history, but it also develops a common language that optimizes the architectural discourse, which is an important part of architectural education. A collection of references works like a specific vocabulary, and strengthens the opportunity to participate in the discussion. It is more practical to use names than a whole chain of descriptions to make comparisons between different possible solutions and syntheses during discussions in courses, at architectural offices, or when judging competition entries. Professor Jerker Lundeqvist said the following, based on Wittgenstein's thoughts on the knowledge of action:

> *When we learn a certain profession, like architecture, for example, we learn to participate in the language game that is part of professional practice. We learn to play the architectural language game by the rules. A major part of professional knowledge is the concepts that you need to know to practice that profession. But there are no clear rules for how you use these concepts; you have to learn that by studying a number of typical cases for which the principles have been used.* (Lundeqvist 1991)

What is typical can be made very clear by using references and comparing them. Drawings and words are the language of architecture, but there is an interplay of language within technology and many other disciplines that an architect has to at least partially master. To work as an architect means to be open-minded and prepared to observe and learn in any situation.

Notes

1 Wittgenstein, Conversation with
M. O´C Drury in 1930 quoted by
Lawson (2008, 287).

2 The Royal Architectural Institute
of Canada is a voluntary national
association established in 1907 as
the voice for architecture and its
practice in Canada.
https://www.raic.org/architecture_
architects/what_is_an_architect/
index_e.htm

3 Writing competition organized by
the European Association for Architectural Education. Years 2003–2005.

4 Syntax is a linguistic term for rules
that describe how you build complex
structures, phrases and sentences
by combining separate units in a
given language.

5 Linton (1996, 104) quoting Bonta:
Architecture and its interpretation
(1979, 64).

6 Erik Reitzel is the structural engi-
neer behind, for example, The Grande
Arche in Paris (1983), designed by
Johan Otto von Spreckelsen.

7 In: Allen et al. (2004).

8 Art museum Ordrupgaard
near Copenhagen.

References

**Allen, Stan; Foster, Hal and Frampton,
Kenneth:** Stocktaking 2004: *Questions
about the Present and Future of Design.*
In: Saunders, William, S. (ed.):
The New Architecural Pragmatism.
A Harvard Design Magazine Reader.
University of Minnesota Press 2007

Anderberg, Thomas: *Alla är vi kritiker.
Om den nödvändiga konsten att
värdera och kritikens osäkra grunder.*
Atlas 2009, 148

Balfour, Alan: *The Architectural
Association.* In: Pearce, Martin; Toy,
Maggie (eds): *Educating Architects.*
Academy Editions, London 1995, 78

Broadbent, Geoffrey: *Architectural
Education.* In: Pearce, Martin; Toy,
Maggie (eds): *Educating Architects.*
Academy Editions, London 1995, 10–17

Forty, Adrian: *Words and Buildings.
A Vocabulary of Modern Architecture.*
Thames & Hudson 2000, 13, 29–41

Graham, Elizabeth Marie: *Studio
Design Critique: Student and Faculty
Expectation and Reality.* A Thesis.
The School of Landscape Architecture.
Christian Brothers University 2003, 2

Hillier, Bill: *Space is the Machine.
A configurational theory of architecture.*

Cambridge University Press 1996, 45–53

Koolhaas, Rem: *Conversations with Students.* Architecture at Rice 30, Princeton Architectural Press 1996, 58–59

Lawson, Bryan: *How Designers Think. The design process demystified.* Architectural Press 2008, 287

Leach, Neil: *Fractures and Breaks.* In: Pearce, Martin; Toy, Maggie (eds): *Educating Architects.* Academy Editions, London 1995, 28

Linn, Björn: *Vad skall arkitekten kunna?* Arkitekttidningen (AT) no. 9/1982, 4–5

Linton, Johan: *Om arkitekturens matematik. En studie av Le Corbusiers Modulor.* Examensarbete, Matematiska Inst. Chalmers Tekniska högskola 1996, 104

Lundberg, Erik: *Arkitekturens föreställningsvärld.* In: *Arkitekturens formspråk,* band 1. Stockholm 1945

Lundeqvist, Jerker: *Arkitektur och språkspel.* Tidskriften Arkitektur 4, 1991

Nervi, Pier Luigi: *Aesthetics and Technology in Building.* Cambridge, MA. 1965, 191

Pallasmaa, Juhani: *Eye, Hand, Head and Heart – Conceptual Knowledge and Tacit Wisdom in Architecture.* In: Villner, L.; Abarkan, A. (eds): *The Four Faces of Architecture—on the dynamics of architectural knowledge.* School of Architecture, The Royal Institute of Technology,

Stockholm 2005

Pérez-Gómez, Alberto: *Built upon Love. Architectural Longing after Ethics and Aesthetics.* The MIT Press, Cambridge, Massachusetts Institute of Technology 2006, 3, 109

Schön, Donald, A.: *The Design Studio. An Exploration of its Traditions and Potentials.* RIBA Publications Limited, London 1985, 3

Scruton, Roger: *The Aesthetics of Architecture.* Methuen & Co. Ltd., London 1979, 240

Silber, John: *Architecture of the Absurd. How "Genius" Disfigured a Practical Art.* The Quantutuck Lane Press, New York 2007, 76

Tschumi, Bernard: *Architecture and Limits* (1980). In: Nesbitt, K. (ed.): *Theorizing a New Agenda for Architecture: An Anthology of Architectural Theory* 1965–1995. Princeton Architectural Press 1996, 152

Utbildningsforum 2011: *Kandidatenkäten 2011.* Studenthandläggare Schuman, Matilda 2011

Vitruvius: *Om arkitektur tio böcker.* Byggförlaget, Stockholm (1.1.3)

Weiner, Frank: *Five Critical Horizons for Architectural Educators in an Age of Distraction.* European Association for Architectural Education. EAAE News Sheet 72/ 2005, 21

4 Can I be an autodidact?

Poetry is a tremendous school of insecurity and uncertainty....
Poetry—writing it as well as reading it—will teach you
humility, and rather quickly at that.

Joseph Brodsky's uncompromising view above, on the significance of poetry, may certainly be applied to architecture, according to Juhani Pallasmaa (2005, 64).

Can I be an autodidact?

There is more or less a consensus that architects need all the skills and knowledge that were described earlier in order to practice their profession. On the other hand, there are differences of opinion about when these proficiencies should be learned, and to what level. Do the students need to master these skills *before* they start design training, or can they discover which types of knowledge they need *during* the design training? In the first scenario, the students will find that their knowledge level increases, even if it may seem abstract and difficult to use. In the second scenario, when the design work itself guides the need for learning, the students can attain a deeper understanding, but their gains in knowledge can be fragmentary. This puts great responsibility on the teachers, on their breadth of knowledge, and on their sensitivity and flexibility. There is also a need to stimulate and, to a certain extent, support the dynamics of the student group.

These pedagogic qualities are also needed for teaching skills like digital techniques, sculpture and freehand drawing that can either be taught as separate subjects or be introduced in conjunction with studio projects.

But do students really absorb all this knowledge and master all these skills? It seems that the feeling of not having learned enough is very common. Several students express this in questionnaires:

I find it very difficult to say what I know and do not know. It is hard to be sure about what level of knowledge is sufficient before trying the career...

...It has been a hard few years, and I'm very unsure of what I really know; my self-confidence is much worse than when I started the program. I would have liked to have had more technical studies, because at least then it's easier to know if you understand it or not, and what you need to learn to be proficient. Theoretical subjects could have been a larger part of the studies, since as it stands, it seems like you have to find out most everything yourself, or just sit and guess, make mistakes, and try again. Before this I studied for three years at a university, and it was quite a lot easier to ascertain what you had to know, and afterwards, you knew what you had actually learned.
(Utbildningsforum 2011)

The alternate method of seeking knowledge—primarily during studio projects—can also be very popular. Architect Zaha Hadid describes her years at the Architectural Association School of Architecture in London as follows:

But there—at AA in 1972, when I started—no one taught you anything: they didn't teach you to draw, they didn't tell you where or what to look at. They didn't explain anything, either. The idea was that there would always be people there who you could go to if you wanted to know something. And there really were always teachers there for what you wanted to learn more about. It was all about creating your own path through the system and understanding what you wanted to get out of it. That takes a long time and therefore you really focus on what you want to achieve with the education.
(Psykoanalytisk Tid/Skrift 2009: 28–29. *Arkitektutbildning*)

Several theorists and practitioners maintain that learning to design is impossible. The Belgian architect Lucien Kroll doubts in frustration if architecture can be taught at all at a higher education level. He calls for some kind of reality-based "workshops" that would deal with real-life problems that students have identified in society. Other architects that are involved with education feel that the most important aspect of both design and architectural training is to pass on the insight that design is an activity in which awareness of *what* you do and *why* you do it is pivotal. However, the most important questions cannot be taught; they must be discovered and their meanings assimilated.

Professor Donald Schön, who was quoted earlier, developed a theory on the importance of reflection in the educational profession, partly from his studies of architectural education. His answers to the question of why design cannot be taught are as follows:

1 You can learn the rules, but they cannot be followed mechanically. To apply them you have to use the art of reflection-in-action.

2 Design is holistic. The final solution is not the sum of the partial solutions.

3 Successful design depends on the designer's ability to discern and appreciate design qualities and relevant concepts (for example, open/closed), which can be learned during the activity of designing.

4 The student perceives something different than what the teacher says; i.e. there can be a disparity between the teacher's intention and the student's perception.

5 Because design is a creative activity that aims to find new solutions, you cannot describe in advance how to do it.

Schön explains how architecture students can gradually adopt a reflective way of thinking; how a process/discussion with a teacher in a studio develops from the teacher's individual relationship to each student. Successively, the student can begin to understand that he or she is expected to learn through action—both to know what design is, and how to do it. Their own ability develops through action—*learning by doing*—and in discussions with a supportive teacher. Other people can help the students, but only when the students begin to understand this mysterious process themselves. Even if others can help them, they are still essentially autodidacts. Schön cites Socrates: *I am afraid it is something that cannot be done by teaching* (Schön 1990, 84). The Portuguese architect Alvaro Siza (2009, 228) explains:

> *Architecture is the unveiling of an obscure and latent collective desire. It cannot be taught, but you can learn to strive for it.... In other words: architecture is uncertainty, and uncertainty demands an impersonal and anonymous wish, the union of subjectivity and objectivity.*

In turn, the Italian architect Giorgio Grassi says that teachers can only instill *awareness* in their students: *This awareness is our only goal at school (it is also my main objective as an architect).* He feels that knowledge of architectural history is especially important, since it helps us to understand our relationship to the present. One can agree with him about the importance of architectural history, but an architectural education should also provide awareness of and insight into the aforementioned fields of knowledge, plus an ethical and aesthet-ic relationship to society and to the lives of its people.

If it is only a question of awareness, do you really need to go through several years of higher education? Couldn't you gain it in some other way in your life? Sometimes people do, indeed, maintain that some famous architects were autodidacts (which is only partly true). For example, Mies van der Rohe did not have any formal architectural education, and Frank Lloyd Wright only studied a few years at a

Le Corbusier started his education to become a watch engraver in his father's and grandfather's footsteps at the age of 14. During his apprenticeship, he made this engraving on a pocket watch for his father. ©F.L.C./BUS 2013

university. Le Corbusier had a short university education, but no architectural degree, and he liked to say that he had no education at all (probably referring to the diploma that he did not have). In reality, he basically had training as a designer of cases for pocket watches and he also had an informal, thorough education (partly self-guided) that included teaching, mentoring, and advice from several competent people.[1] None of these three famous architects started their architectural careers without any education, and all of them had a comprehensive knowledge of materials from working with craftsmen or master builders from an early age (in the case of Mies van der Rohe and Le Corbusier, their fathers).

You could say that their education followed the traditional apprentice model, supplemented with some university courses. Obviously, they were also extremely gifted artistically, and, according to several biographers, very ambitious and self-confident. Today, now that handcrafts have diminished because of a more industrial building process, such an education is more difficult to attain and rather unusual.

It would be hard to become an architect as an autodidact in today's world without the foundation that handcrafts and/or accepted standards of beauty could contribute earlier, especially without an awareness of the basic concepts of architecture. It would probably be as difficult as trying to be an autodidact in another profession without any higher education. Sometimes master builders even construct relatively complex buildings without the expertise of an architect, but usually these are what Tschumi would categorize as *buildings* and not *architecture*. There are examples of engineers who have succeeded in combining their technical skills with the architect's characteristic holistic and aesthetic thinking, but they are the exceptions. On the other hand, there are hardly any examples of practicing architects who started their careers as architectural theorists. Sometimes people mention Ludwig Wittgenstein's famous Stonborough House (1926–1928) in Vienna as an example of how a philosopher can act as a successful architect, but Wittgenstein trained as an engineer and he designed the villa for his sister in

The Wittgenstein House (a.k.a. the Stonborough House) built
in 1928 in Vienna for Ludvig Wittgenstein's sister. Designed
by Wittgenstein and architect Paul Engelmann.
Photo: Jadwiga Krupinska

cooperation with the architect Paul Engelmann.

The students' anxiety that they don't know what they are learning generates uncertainty, and that is precisely contrary to the overriding goal of education—which is to instill the courage to formulate professional, and always partly subjective, judgments. For the most part, this anxiety is caused by not knowing that architectural knowledge is added like layers of sediment, rather than being constructed systematically. Finding this out at the onset of the education would help, but you can build awareness of the specific character of architectural studies in various ways.

One example is to involve older students in the younger students' education, which we did for several years in our teaching in Stockholm. Beginning students in year 1 could invite students in year 4 to act as "junior assistants", who would complement, not replace, the normal assistants' work in the design studios. The students were free to pair up more or less randomly, and decide when, where and how often they would meet to discuss the year 1 students' projects. This activity became popular very quickly, and practically all of the year 4 students were involved. The younger students felt that it was easier to "open up" to the year 4 students and, for example, ask them about obscure words. They seemed less distant than the usual teachers, who could easily be seen as authorities due to their professional experience. The year 4 students, for their part, felt that acting as junior assistants was difficult in the beginning, but they soon discovered that when they had to answer questions like *why* certain things are done, and *what* is important, they verbalized their tacit knowledge and were surprised that they had learned much more than they thought during their studies. "*My own words take me by surprise and teach me what I think*" said Derrida, quoted by Adrian Forty (2000). Even the teachers felt that group work and discussions about architecture had developed because of the junior assistant program.

The knowledge and skills you learn at architecture school are not sufficient. Observation and reflection must be the architect's constant companions both while studying and later, in professional practice. The architect has to be sensitive *outwardly* to learn continually about life, techniques, colors in the landscape or the silence of darkness, and be sensitive *inwardly* for reflection and perception. In that sense, an architect *is* an autodidact with a constant need to learn.

The curriculum

The uncertainty at the onset of architecture studies could be alleviated somewhat if architectural education began with massive and intense training in essential subjects like construction materials and methods, statics, building physics and architectural history, so that the knowledge of these subjects could be applied later in the design studio. That would at least give the student a catalog of answers, but it can also endanger the pedagogical goals if periodic practical training exercises are not included. An overload of rational and normative restrictions can inhibit design sketches. The fact is that students who begin studying architecture after completing an engineering degree often have difficulties in transitioning to design. They tend to concentrate on the product's "correctness" and do not allow themselves to be as open and playful as their inexperienced classmates when formulating possible design solutions. On the other hand, technical knowledge of buildings can be a source of inspiration instead of an inhibition if the student realizes that exact details are not the starting point for design work.

In the early stages of their education, students need mostly broad, applied knowledge, plus training and experiments that they can relate to, rather than extensive theoretical studies. It is interesting to note that a curriculum utilizing this type of principle was used at the Bauhaus, in which students did a few years of composition and material studies in glass, mural painting, ceramics, metal and other materials before they began studying architectural design.

A curriculum that intends to encourage creativity should, according to psychologist Anne Bore (2006), consider the typical sequence in the development of creative skills in terms of psychological findings. It should be based on a model consisting of four conceptual phases. These phases are processes of: *uncertainty, visioning, realization and readiness. Uncertainty* is described as *"grappling with ambiguity of circumstances necessary for creativity".* Many students struggle at this stage, since they feel that their own mental state is chaotic. It is this uncertainty that emerges in the students' voices heard earlier. Gradually, though, all kinds of possible ideas begin to materialize when the students dare to rely on subjectivity or when, as psychologists say, they "open themselves to their inner landscape", in the *visioning* phase. Then, during the *realization* phase, ideas are tested and choices made. Finally, during the *readiness* phase, the structure appears, decisions are easier, the uncertainty dissipates, and it is fun to work. "Opening yourself to your inner landscape" is basically a matter of trusting your own experiences, emotions, and knowledge. It is an essential stage in becoming a skilled designer.

Associate Professor of Architecture at the University of Texas Stephen Temple describes several levels in the development of a designer's professional skill, namely *experiential, cognitive, associative* and *autonomous.*[2] At the *experiential* level, which applies to most first-year students and some second-year students, learning occurs primarily through playful exploration and repetition. The following *cognitive* level is characterized by, simply put, a gradual structuring of one's own experiences, utilizing new knowledge, and developing strategies for conscious choices. The *associative* level connotes that the sensory, spatial and symbolic are conceptualized from experience. At this level, the ability to discern which experiences need acting upon increases. Finally, the *autonomous* level is reached when one can act independently, aware of one's own motives and goals. To become skilled, a designer must undergo a developmental and psychological transformation from the experiential level to the autonomous. But the process does not stop there; skills continue to develop. Getting into phase with the different stages is individual. Often, the student gains insight later in their education.

In 1983, the psychologist Howard Gardner published his book *Frames of Mind—The Theory of Multiple Intelligences*, which has had a very big impact on how we view intelligence and pedagogy. Gardner described seven different types of intelligence, namely: linguistic, musical, logical-mathematical, spatial, bodily-kinesthetic, interpersonal (social) and intrapersonal (introspective).[3] The boundaries between these types can often be indistinct. Individuals can be intelligent in several ways depending on their inherited abilities, but also through playing, study and practice. Normally though, one or more types of intelligence are predominant. Western civilization has esteemed the mathematical-logical and linguistic intelligences, in contrast to the rest, causing them to be strongly promoted.

Gardner states that a curriculum should be universal at an abstract level, but the teaching should be flexible and adapted to each individual. In his argument, he makes a distinction between subject matter and subject perception, and he recommends an educational environment that can stimulate all types of intelligence. A professor of design methodology, Nigel Cross, who has investigated the way in which many designers work, says that design skills are found in several of Gardner's intelligence types. Thus, design should be considered a *separate and special type of intelligence*, which would help in developing design education.

It is of course tempting to think how much an individual's opportunities can expand if he or she gets the *encouragement* and possibility to use several kinds of intelligence. That is the situation for an architect if he or she wants to master a modern version of Vitruvius' criteria: *firmitas, utilitas, venustas*. In reality, architectural education is primarily an illustration of Gardner's pedagogical ideas: a broad overview of subject matter, with attention to the individual in the project studios. This teaching method is dependent on the teacher's understanding and awareness, plus the instruction hours available for involving themselves in each student's development.

The experiential level

Stephen Temple is aware of the psychological processes described above when he explains the problems involved with having teachers from the upper years, or practitioners, teaching in the first year. In the upper years, the teachers focus on conveying professional *skills*, and they often do the same with first-year students, not realizing that they are at a different level in terms of design proficiency. That which can motivate higher year students does not apply to beginner-level students. The goal should be to encourage the younger students to take risks based on their own subjective views.

In design work, as in other creative work, people can be hindered by mental blocks. Sometimes students lose control of and belief in their own abilities. Their self-confidence evaporates and a feeling of vulnerability and a forced dependency can cause a defensive attitude. However, the difficulties these students experience do not necessarily indicate a lack of talent or creativity, which is a common judgment. While teaching, I noticed that problems like this can appear because:

1 It takes some time before the students learn that you have to switch over from the linear thought process that was predominant in earlier studies, to one of analyzing through synthesis. This insight does not always occur in the first year, and the maturing process is different for each student.

2 Students can have a strong self-critical attitude, which prevents them from taking any risk, for fear of possible failure. This can lead to an inhibited and sometimes paralyzed attitude in relation to design work. It can be helpful and liberating to learn that their own sketches can be revised or rejected; that they may just be valid for a few hours or a few days. Mental blocks in design work can be caused by both too little knowledge and too much!

It is common in years 1–3 at many architecture schools that students—in groups of approximately 20—work individually on their first design projects. One or two teachers are available for help a few afternoons each week. The teaching is somewhat coordinated for the whole first-year group because it is important to introduce fundamental concepts. Teachers have quite a lot of leeway, within a certain framework, to interpret the curriculum according to their own interests and temperaments. Most higher level schools of architecture have curricula that are similar in terms of methods and content, but there can be differences in the scope and timing of the various subjects and skills. Normally, for example, urban planning is offered at higher levels because of its complexity, but there are exceptions. At an international conference on architectural education, one European school of architecture revealed that the first assignment for their students in year one was to create a city plan. The explanation was that all students had their own experience of what a city is. Naturally, the students lacked the skills and tools for a deeper investigation, but the exercise did show them the intricacy of urban design problems and the work of the architect. Such an introduction to architectural education is unconventional, but the head teacher felt that it was a success, both for skill-building and for insights into the design process.[4]

For my own courses when teaching the first year, I thought that the most important objective was to inspire the students' awareness of architectonic space, to encourage three-dimensional thought, and to impart the bravery to tread on uncertain ground. It became clear that the students needed different amounts of time to assimilate the new thought processes needed for design and to relate simultaneously to previous experiences. The goal was to help the students to gradually increase their awareness and possibly attain what Juhani Pallasmaa calls existential wisdom. As head of the first-year program, I could contribute throughout the year by introducing short (hour-long) design sketches, during which the students would often be surprised by their own discoveries. One student could be exultant when they found the strange beauty of a 17.5-degree angle, or another student could suddenly shriek in amazement: *Everything is space!* Short assignments were alternated with longer projects that gave time for reflection. I realized that teaching was a composition of knowledge and skills, where a changing rhythm during the course year was as important as that in a piece of music.

One assignment that was repeated for the first-year students for several years was "A space by the water", a time for the students to engage subjectively and emotionally in both the practical and poetic/ sensory aspects. Contemplations about the meaning of water, the concept of "rest", and room/space were the important aspects. This was also the first training in seeking knowledge for an independent solution, making a physical model, and summarizing the proposal with illustrations. One student, who could not attend the critique, left a written account of the working process:

> *This project is called "A space by the water" and I assume that most of us have had different experiences of water and that we store these impressions inside us—as emotional memories and imagery. One of my images is the steep cliff at Millesgården dropping down to the water's edge. Just think of having a little room there, hidden, but so close to the center of Stockholm. Another image is a Plexiglas tent, supported by wires and chromed pipe above the sand dunes on Sweden's west coast. The third image is of large, glittering gold spheres that I saw while travelling along the coast of Jylland in Denmark.*

These glittering spheres, with their golden reflections, provided inspiration and a concept:

> *One of the term's first lectures was about domes. From my notes I realized that I could build my model with a specific kind of triangles. I would make these triangles out of Plexiglas.*

The journey continues with the problems of locating the right Plexiglas, visiting building information centers to find manufacturers of spiral staircases and the plastic sheets that are used for greenhouses, and searching, unsuccessfully, for relevant books on how to build domes, etc. Eventually, there was an insight that the pattern of a standard soccer ball could be used as a model. The decision was made to build a model with pentagons and hexagons and their halves. What followed was making triangle templates and visiting a glazier to learn how to cut glass. The student also describes how he considered different mirrors and angles to create the beautifully silvery-golden shimmering surface that he wanted. He then took a step back to examine the placement of the dome on the site once more. Finally, he explained the sensual experiences that the dome could give, both outside and inside. He utilized his own experiences to create new meanings.

Working toward autonomy level in the design studio

In higher level classes, the teaching is done in relatively autonomous studios, usually with 15 to 20 students who normally work in the same studio for the final two years. The design projects depend on the focus of the studio. These can include advanced design, landscape architecture, urban design, building in extreme conditions, etc. In recent decades the subject emphasis in many studios has been strong-ly influenced by a growing interest in environmental issues and sustainability, and in terms of methods, by the digital revolution.

Design studios can be based on a fixed brief which is often derived from real-world situations, but there can also be "open" topics which start with societal problems that have been identified by the students. The question of whether the projects should be based on reality, and if so, to what level, is often an issue for discussion. For instance, in the North Studio at Wesleyan University, Connecticut, students work on small real-world projects in architecture and landscape, together with non-profit and public entities (Huge 2009, 65). The students work with design, collaborate with consultants, and also build their proposals. Another example is the pedagogical method in architectural education at Cape Peninsula University in South Africa, where they concentrate on providing solutions for social problems. Designing and building an outside space with a roof of polycarbonate sheets improved the entry conditions at

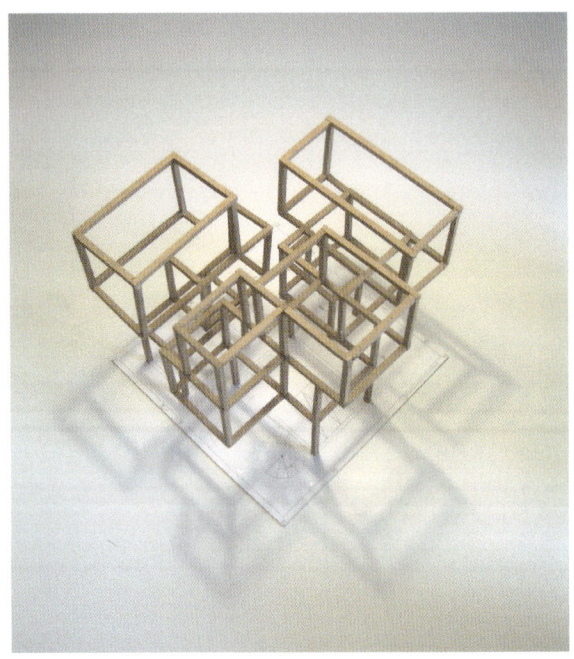

Spatial studies. Examples of studio work. Photo: Jadwiga Krupinska

a primary school.[5] In some countries, studio work can be applied to real projects that the school administrates for a practicing professor. In that case, the studio functions like a real architectural office, but any income goes to the school.[6]

The widespread use of digital techniques and availability of information on the Internet (i.e. maps, information on building materials, contact with centers of innovation and professional knowledge around the world) have both become indispensable supplements to traditional tools. Knowledge of the actual subjects is taught in the studio in lectures, seminars, or through Internet research, and is strengthened by short, explanatory exercises before undertaking more comprehensive design projects. There are also periodic critique sessions.

The design studio culture is characterized by a particular viewpoint and working method. The teaching is shaped by the head professor and the teachers in the studio, and can, in fact, have aspects of the apprentice system. There are also studios that may be seen as contemporary versions of the traditional Beaux Arts studio model.

The emphasis on different values may vary. For example, in one studio, the focus can be on conceptual thinking, but technical in another. Ethical discussions are very important when planning a project and when investigating problems. In a design studio, the student internalizes values and standards that can be invaluable for their future profession. In the studio you learn architectonic design by *doing*, according to the *analysis by synthesis method*, which is explained in the next chapter. Students work independently and individually, although group projects may be used for subtopics. In addition, a further aspect of the culture of the design studio is, according to a report by The American Institute of Architecture Students (AIAS 2006), that it retains the myth of the absolute authority of the studio critics, the long work days and late nights, a focus on schematic solutions, and a lack of discussion with users.

The long days and late nights of work may be a sign that architecture students and teachers place too much emphasis on the product presentation—the final proposal—and less on the actual design process. With an emphasis on the process, the working method would come into focus, rather than the completed proposal. On the other hand, the hard work is partly due to the fact that many students find a challenge in the design aspect; the challenge of seeking the optimal solution, even though you eventually learn that frustrations and uncertainties can lurk along the path.

Students generally have a strong *inner motivation* that drives them. Research in pedagogy shows such inner motivation to be a more important factor in completing tasks than external motivation, which is related to rewards and grades. Therefore, the kind of intense competition that was de rigueur at the École Royale des Beaux Arts is not desirable. Quite the contrary, the learning environment in a studio should provide ample opportunity for students to learn from each other. Students arrive at the studio with a variety of experiences and knowledge which can, if utilized properly, influence the teaching in a positive way. It can be everything from presentation techniques to technical aspects. A well-organized studio should strive to gradually increase the student's awareness of how to deal with the complexity of architecture.

There are teachers who are convinced that an architect must start by learning as much as possible about the specific field of work, for example, housing, health care, etc. The idea is that a thorough analysis of these facts and the corresponding data can provide a starting point for design. However, students can overdo the search for facts, complete a deep analysis of the research, and then have no time (or courage) to develop the design itself. On the whole, meticulous, traditional, analysis work is a secure albeit time-consuming activity. That cannot be said of synthesizing, where you expose your own subjectivity to confrontation. To alternate quickly between analysis and synthesis is often risky, since the same material can be interpreted in different ways. The formulation of a synthesis demands that the student makes subjective judgments as well as choices. When the analysis part takes precedence, it may mean that the student wants to escape to the (fictive) security of research and data. Reaching an overview and engaging in comprehensive holistic thinking can be difficult when you are diving deeper into new domains of expertise and their levels of detail. Unfortunately, the design work can thus diverge on two disparate, disconnected paths: a deep analysis and an ad hoc synthesis.

There are also teachers who maintain the view that the actual process of design generates questions that inspire deeper studies. During the initial sketching phase, the student recognizes the need for new skills or of developing old ones. For instance, it could be about specific building materials for a proposal or the width of access roads, etc. The creative work, to seek a holistic design, is simultaneously a search engine for learning. You seek your way forward by sketching possible solutions.

The attempts that were described earlier to rationalize the design process have been abandoned. The more or less traditional design process and the architect's intuitive method (see Chapters 5 and 6) are accepted practice. In the process of *doing*, knowledge and skill is utilized, as well as one's own experiences. The student becomes train-ed in the ability to discern important aspects—what is relevant or irrelevant—providing the skill to formulate concepts and contemplate possible solutions. The students' proposals are *summaries* of complex interrelationships. These summaries consist of elements containing important aspects of *firmitas, utilitas* and *venustas.*

This work expresses both theoretical aspects and practical skills. You also learn and apply new tools like visualization and illustration. Developing and communicating ideas through drawings and models can be another new experience for many students, as is this new language, namely a language that alternates between graphic and verbal representations. Professional concepts like *scale, form* or *design language* are assimilated. Through practice, the students learn to "think architecturally" (Ledewitz 1985), which requires flexible thinking and being aware of physical, symbolic and poetic aspects as in the process of sketching (see Chapter 5). The use of the studio as a teaching environment is a complex answer to the complexity of the design process. In the studio there should be no boundaries; there should be the freedom to play with an array of solutions; everything is worth trying. The ideal situation is to be simultaneously playful and serious, an attitude that John Dewey describes as the most desirable for creative work:

> *To be playful and serious at the same time is possible, and it defines the ideal mental condition. Absence of dogmatism and prejudice, presence of intellectual curiosity and flexibility, are manifest in the free play of the mind upon a topic. To give the mind this free play is not to encourage toying with a subject, but is to be interested in the unfolding of the subject on its own account, apart from its subservience to a preconceived belief or habitual aim. Mental play is open-mindedness, faith in the power of thought to preserve its own integrity without external supports and arbitrary restrictions.* (Dewey 1997, 219)

Design exercises are included in each school year and they reinforce the working method. The assignments vary: in one studio you may design a library, in the next, housing, but the method is the same. Concurrently, and parallel to the design work, the students gain factual knowledge in technical subjects and humanities, and skills and awareness of which factors to consider when making design choices. Finding a good solution that meets the requirements of the problem (which may have been reformulated during the design work) is joyful and empowering. The process is composite and depends to a great extent on the control and the mastery of given variables, but also on the capacity for self-control. This is one of the reasons why architecture students are very motivated and hard-working.

Mastering complexity

When you write an essay for a humanities course, you use words to discuss and illustrate your thoughts. There is leeway for the reader's different perceptions and interpretations. In a technical or scientific course, the answers should instead be unequivocal. After learning axioms and formulas, the students build a relatively stable foundation. They have a chance to study long enough to master the subject material and reach the level of an expert. However, an architecture student is more vulnerable; his or her field of expertise is always strewn with inexperience traps, but it is also open to creativity and playfulness. Every situation is new; every project is different. Paradoxically, uncertainty is the basis for continuous self-development, since "you always have to break new ground" as one student puts it in Lisa Wingård's study.

The Finnish architectural theorist Juhani Pallasmaa says that when you are discussing architecture and the interaction between theory, research, practice and education, a distinction must be made between *instrumental knowledge*, or skills, on the one hand, and *existential knowledge*, or wisdom, on the other. The former can be the subject of theory and research, and can be taught and quite effectively included in architectural education, but the latter, existential knowledge, is quite different. It can be added to life experiences and problem interpretation, thus becoming part of the individual's self-identity. Nonetheless, to learn existential wisdom is difficult, if not impossible, despite it being essential to every artistic endeavor. It can grow along with the individual's personal development and under the influence of the teacher's personality traits. With this explanation, Pallasmaa illustrates the knowledge types that were defined by Aristotle, and he describes their roles in architecture: *Epistéme*, scientific, independent of context; *Techne*, skills and crafts, based on experience; and *Phronesis*, practical wisdom.

It is quite possible that the students quoted in Chapter 1 misunderstood their teachers when they became disoriented and frightened at the moment they were told to forget most of what they had learned and come to the studio "naked". On the contrary, all life experiences can contribute to the development of existential knowledge—Phronesis—and thus to professional awareness. At several architecture schools, student experiences from other fields than architecture are activated as a way for them to relate more directly to important architectonic issues, such as individual or multi-family housing, perceiving human scale, the scale of buildings, etc. The exercises are often based on everyday problems so that the students can widen their own frames of reference and, with the help of teachers, learn to evaluate conventions and standards with a critical eye. It is not evident from the student questionnaires quoted in Chapter 1 and elsewhere, however, that they are aware of the aspect of the architectural education that is so new and so hard to grasp— namely *a new way of thinking*. This must be assimilated in order to work with design.

Specific subject knowledge from different disciplines and skills as well as life experience is necessary to create architecture that respects the basic concepts of *firmitas, utilitas, venustas* (durability, function, beauty) in every object you design. None of those fundamental Vitruvian aspects can be ignored, and each one requires considerable skill. Architecture that is beautiful but not functional or durable is not good enough, and durable buildings that lack ethical and aesthetic aspects can hardly be considered architecture. Beyond this, the architect needs real-life experience to evaluate the needs and situations of people locally and in society at large.

Designing—the complex consolidation of knowledge, skills and experiences—contains exploration and can be compared in some ways to the work of a researcher. However, a practitioner differs from an abstract theorist in at least two distinct aspects. First, he or she must constantly synthesize all of their personal knowledge and experience, and simultaneously calculate the risks and consequences of each intervention. Second, every concrete situation involves a confrontation with the world as a totality of time and space, interlaced with historical roots and social and cultural structures. This totality, as described by Professor of Social Planning Richard Bolan, also includes objective understanding and subjective awareness, without the luxury of abstraction or categorization.

It may be said that architects work in a *constant state of uncertainty* because they can never master all of the necessary skills before starting a project. To practice their profession, they have to learn to cope with these uncertainties and work past them in order to make the right decisions:

> *there is always someone who has more knowledge within the*
> *specific disciplines that architecture encompasses. Despite that, it*
> *is the task of the architect to formulate the best holistic solution.*
> (Tham and Videgård Hansson in a discussion with Johan
> Linton. Psykoanalytisk Tid/Skrift 2009: 28–29)

To control the complexity that is implicit in design work and in their field of knowledge, architects have to cultivate their professional acumen by thinking openly and critically. Their education *does not* strive to create a secure situation without uncertainty, because uncertainty is inherent in creative work. Instead, the goal is that the students learn to deal with uncertainties so that they can be used constructively, and that they gain the ability to evaluate problems and also to criticize their own proposals creatively. To reach that level, training in both critical thinking and critical work methods, together with the ability to question program briefs and standard and conventional relationships, is essential. This is all part of the architect's professional practice, and can now be explained with the latest findings from design theory.

Above: Tree hotel, interior. Designed by Tham & Videgård
Arkitekter and completed in 2011 in Harads, Sweden.

Opposite: Tree hotel, Tham & Videgård Arkitekter. The hotel room
is a cube, four meters on each side. The cladding of mirrored glass
makes the cube at one with nature. Photo: Åke E:son Lindman

Notes

References

1 According to Linton (2009, 339). Le Corbusier was very critical of the architectural education of his day and he proposed several times that the Beaux Arts schools should be closed.

2 Based on the book *The Psychology of Skill* by psychologist Phillip D. Tomporowski.

3 Gardner later added two more types of intelligence to the original list, namely nature and existential intelligence.

4 Stated during an international conference on education issues, Torino 1994.

5 According to the seminar with architect Hermie E Voulgarelis, June 2012.

6 This was the situation at the Tokyo Institute of Technology during our visit in 2005.

AIAS: *The Redesign of Studio Culture.* A Report of the AIAS Studio Culture Task Force. The American Institute of Architecture Students 2006, 5

Bolan, Richard S.: *The Practitioner as Theorist. The Phenomenology of the Professional Episode.* APA Journal of the American Planning Association, Vol. 46, July 1980, 261–274

Bore, Anne: *Bottom-up for Creativity in Science? A collaborative model for curriculum and professional development.* Journal of Education for Teaching (JET), Vol. 32, No. 4, November 2006, 413–422

Cross, Nigel: *The Nature and Nurture of Design Ability.* Design Studies, Vol. 11, No. 3, July 1990, 134

Dewey, John: *How We Think.* Dover Publications INC 1997 (1910), 219

Forty, Adrian: *Words and Buildings. A Vocabulary of Modern Architecture.* Thames & Hudson 2000, 33

Gardner, Howard: *Frames of Mind —The Theory of Multiple Intelligences.* Fontana Press 1993 (1983)

Grassi, Giorgio: *An opinion on architectural education and the conditions our profession has to work on.*

Domus No. 714, March 1990

Huge, Elijah: *Study as a Course of Practice: The Work of North Studio at Wesleyan University.* Journal of Architectural Education, Vol. 62/3, 2009, 65

Kroll, Lucien; Mikellides, Byron: *Can Architecture Be Taught?* Journal of Architectural Education, Vol. 35, No. 1, Fall 1981, 36–39

Ledewitz, Stefani: *Models of Design in Studio Teaching.* Journal for Architectural Education, Vol. 38, No. 2, 1985, 2

Linton, Johan: *Institutionen och ensamheten. Le Corbusiers arkitektutbildning.* In: Psykoanalytisk Tid/Skrift 2009: 28–29.

Pallasmaa, Juhani: *Eye, Hand, Head and Heart – Conceptual Knowledge and Tacit Wisdom in Architecture.* In: Villner, L.; Abarkan, A. (eds): *The Four Faces of Architecture— On the Dynamics of Architectural Knowledge.* School of Architecture, The Royal Institute of Technology, Stockholm 2005

Psykoanalytisk Tid/Skrift 2009: 28-29. *Arkitekturskola. Bolle Tham och Martin Videgård Hansson i samtal med Johan Linton,* 336

Psykoanalytisk Tid/Skrift 2009: 28-29. *Arkitektutbildning— Architectural Association. Zaha Hadid i samtal med Richard Levene &*

Fernando Márquez Cecilia, 243–256

Schön, Donald A.: *Educating the Reflective Practitioner. Toward a New Design for Teaching and Learning in the Professions.* Jossey-Bass Publishers, San Francisco 1990 (1986), 84–93, 159–166

Siza, Àlvaro: *Om pedagogik.* Psykoanalytisk Tid/Skrift 2009: 28-29, 228

Temple, Stephen: *A Curriculum Based on the Psychology of Skill: Collaborating with Instructors with Disdain for Teaching Beginning Design.* National Conference on the Beginning Design Student, Atlanta, March 2008 (draft)

Utbildningsforum 2011: *Kandidatenkäten 2011.* Studenthandläggare Matilda Schuman

Wingård, Lisa: *Om att bli arkitekt.* Examensarbete Chalmers Arkitektur 2004/2005, 62

5 The design process

What is design?

It is said that architectural education is somewhat like a "black box" because students enter as laymen and exit as architects, without really knowing what happened in between. Words are used such as "a secret, a mystery", without questioning if there is a secret, and if so, what kind of mystery it is.

Steve Jobs, the late co-founder and CEO of Apple Computer, once said:

> *Design is a funny word. Some people think design means how it looks. But of course, if you dig deeper, it's really how it works.... To design something really well, you have to get it. You have to really grok what it's all about.* (Wolf 1996)

The word "design" has had many different meanings throughout the years. It comes from the Italian word *disegno* (drawing) and was first used in English in the 17th century. Now it is used for both products and their conception in the fields of product design, architecture, and other disciplines that are characterized by creative production, including the engineering profession as well as in art. Design as a verb is the activity of conceptualizing and creating, while the noun can denote the final product.

Design theorist Jerker Lundeqvist notes that there are many meanings of the Latin word *designare,* includes: to mark out, designate, or reveal a sign.

> *Actually, the concept means that a designer designates which qualities a product needs in order to help future users solve a given problem. Design is thus an overall term for many different specific types of design, for example: architectural, graphic, and urban design. Even Industrial Engineering is a type of design.*

To really understand what designers do, you have to include a prefix, like the ones mentioned. (Lundequist 1995, 61)

The idea of design arose in 19th century England at the confluence of industry and the decorative arts. It became more defined in Germany in the early 1900s, was further developed in the USA, and then returned on a broad front to Europe. The concept spread quickly, but the word itself caused some protests. There were proposals in France to replace the term *design* with *stylique* to protect the French linguistic tradition, and even as late as 2010, the French national statistics agency, INSEE, considered replacing *design* with *concept* and *designer* with *concepteur* (Vial 2011).

"Design" is now used for various ways of creating objects, but usually it describes the aesthetic aspects. This could be a remnant of the former polarization between "design" and "construction". In the 1700s, these two concepts were considered to be two aspects of the same activity: namely architecture, according to Adrian Forty.[1] This remained the same during the 1800s, but the concepts began to be delineated at the start of the next century. Architecture as a whole started to be seen as a dichotomy, with thoughts and the immaterial on one side and materials and construction on the other. According to Donald Schön, the English word "designing" connotes the designer's negotiations with the real materials involved in each situation.

The notion of "design" was pivotal in the aforementioned transition of architectural education from primarily apprenticeships with practicing architects, to studies at universities and institutes. The word "design", in itself, made it permissible for the architectural discipline to be *thought*, instead of learned through experience, and this encouraged intellectual input in creative processes. Design in architectural practice is a process of connecting all the parts and details that are included in the concepts of durability, utility and beauty into a convincing, buildable entity. The process itself is a learning experience, necessary for solving each specific design problem. *Learning is the essence of the design process.*[2]

Project work in architectural education and in architectural practice is the act of *independently comprehending a complex situation* to arrive at a new evaluation of a *problem* and, despite uncertainty, finding convincing solutions in the form of proposals for new buildings and facilities. In other words, it involves design—a creative endeavor of translating initially vague ideas and imagined forms into solid, buildable representations. Aspects that make up the intricate whole can be functional requirements, layouts, construction, materials, site conditions, light and color as well as poetic or symbolic expressions, etc. The legendary Bauhaus teacher László Moholy-Nagy emphasized the necessity of a harmonious balance among all the elements required to satisfy functions. Design is *thinking in relationships*. Identifying these relationships and thinking about them generates a need to learn more.

The skills and knowledge, described earlier, that an architect needs for the profession are woven together in the synthesis of designing. This is a mysterious activity for many students, and difficult to comprehend because it requires a different way of thinking than what they are accustomed to from other schools. Becoming aware of how this method is applied, and how useful it is, must be a central purpose of architectural education.

Do architects have a working method?

In the scientific subjects, receptive students (which most architecture students are; see Chapter 8) can reach a certain confidence in dealing with facts, references and formulas. Students can also become confident in their technical skills. This is especially notable when some students can be helped by digital presentations if they are not naturals at free-hand drawing and graphic design. Nonetheless, theoretical knowledge and training in the use of tools are just aids in design work—both very important, yet they do not guarantee the ability to design. Theory courses, intellectualizing and verbal descriptions can give an understanding of the concepts, but *they do not give you an understanding of how you do something.*

Initially, a student has to start designing before they know how to do so. *Some students never understand what the coach is talking about,* says Donald Schön.[3] The reason may be that a student, after primary and secondary school, may have a hard time grasping that to learn the design process you have to start thinking differently. A linear thought progression from analysis to synthesis is rarely successful, since you can hardly predict entirely which variables are important (there are far too many). You approach the complexity of a design problem by suggesting possible solutions and then checking their validity against certain criteria. Unfortunately, there is no complete advance list of criteria; they sometimes only emerge during the project. To understand this special method of periodic re-evaluation, which can give a deeper comprehension, and possibly, a new take on the problem, can be difficult even after year 1. Also, the student often does not know that the choice of preliminary solutions is always a subjective act. Exposing your subjectivity can feel risky, because you reveal your own personality and thus become vulnerable.

Architects often believe that they don't have a specialized work method. For example, the very experienced practitioner Armand Björkman says:

> *It is strange that you can be sketching for so many years without feeling the urge to know how you do it. The only time you actually think about it at all is when you are filing some materials and find 10-year old drawings. Did I really do this?*
> (Björkman 1988, 9)

This is surprising, because Donald Schön's extensive studies of architectural education and his descriptions of the architect's working methods had a great impact on pedagogic thinking around the world. His concept *reflective practitioner* explains the development of the architect's professional competence, which is a mix of technical knowledge and an artistic way of thinking.

Perhaps the reason that architects are not aware of their own method is that it becomes so natural and self-evident that you don't reflect on it once you have learned it—even though *reflection-in-action* is at its core. The hyphenated spelling of Schön's famous concept indicates that the words do not describe separate processes; they must progress simultaneously.

Mapping the design process

A scientific, systematic, way of looking at the design process became necessary when researchers began to investigate design methodology over 50 years ago. Early attempts to describe how designers' creative ideas develop were based on the paradigm prevalent in the 1960s and 1970s. Functionalist and then structuralist thought had spread to most areas and levels of building. Not only were cities planned in terms of separate zones for workplaces and housing; buildings were also divided according to the functions of the separate components, like wind protection, insulation, etc. How they worked together was less understood. Also, different human functions were thought to be segregated in time and space.

The research efforts were driven by the desire to mold design into a branch of science and replace conventional activities with new ones, based on technical logic. This original goal may well have been a rational one considering the earlier view of design as an inexplicable, mysterious act. The theories about how the design process works were based, in keeping with the times, on attempts to divide it up into apparently readable parts. There was an awareness that it included analysis, synthesis and evaluation, and they were viewed as being parts of a more or less linear progression. The belief was that designers start by collecting information, analyzing it, and then combining the results into a synthesis. This was soon rejected as an incorrect model.

In the 1960s researchers wanted to investigate the design process by using the designers' own descriptions of the way they worked, which was a questionable method, since writing is not a designer's normal way of communicating. As the artist Sölve Olsson stated, it's hard for artists and architects to be creative and to simultaneously observe their own creativity. When work is going well, you are so engaged in it that you don't think about *how* you do it, and when work is going badly, you have a split personality: one working; one watching. That is when you scrutinize the process.

The opportunities for insight into the creative process seem to be in reverse proportion to the creative intensity. Knowledge of how creativity does not work is more available than how it does. The health of creativity is still and silent. (Olsson 1989, p. 95)

Renewed research efforts in the 1970s brought designers into the laboratory. Their work process was observed during what were thought to be objective and controlled conditions. Comparisons were also done with the working methods of other professions. Later, in the 1990s, the research was done in the real environment of the design studio. The designers were asked about how they worked, but their answers were hard to make sense of. The researchers tried to find out and map what was going on in the minds of the designers, but they could not get any clear results. They had hoped to be able to use the research to help rationalize the design process and apply the results to constructing intelligent computers.

Various schemas have been presented through the years. For example, the British architectural association RIBA included a summary in their handbook which divides the design process into four phases: "assimilation, general study, development, and communication" with the comment that there can be jumps and feedback between these four phases. The schema by architects Markus and Maver showed the interdependence of the phases, with alternation from analysis and synthesis, to evaluation, and back again, throughout the process.

Jerker Lundequist has delineated three generations of the relatively new field of research in design. The first is a belief that the design process can be categorized as a rational problem-solving method, including analysis, synthesis, evaluation and decision. This viewpoint was characterized by a firm belief in rational analysis and this caused segmentation of the design process. It was agreed rather quickly that a systematic method description like this was over-simplified and did not represent the true design process. The idea that the different design phases are separated and follow a fixed sequence seemed more and more dubious.

In the second generation of design research, the previous linear model was replaced with models based on the idea that the process might not initiate with analysis, but perhaps with a proposed solution and criteria from a client. Design began to be seen as a dialectic process. *"The designer would no longer be an objective expert, but instead, a pedagogue who could bring forth the user's ideas and needs"* (Lundequist 1995, 71). User planning and participation became key concepts, but this was no guarantee of quality, since the users often thought of the short term, while the designers thought long term. Attempts to describe requirements objectively and then develop the design process on a rational foundation have generally failed.

The research projects presented in the first and second generation of design research were theoretical in nature. Their formulation was seemingly based on the desire to reach logical and systematic connections, and not on the actual meaning of observations. It became clear that it was not possible to ascertain if designers really work in a systematic way. You could not rely on their recollections or notes, either. It was uncertain if the designers' journals or their interview answers that were used in various studies were not painting an idealized picture of their working methods to make a good impression on the client. They could have also thought that their descriptions should match certain expectations.

The reason that you cannot explain design with a simple diagram is that it is a very individual, multi-dimensional and exceedingly complex creative process. One example is that a design problem may include different variables that cannot be evaluated using the same units of measurement. Value judgments seem to be unavoidable and they are very difficult to interpret objectively enough to satisfy scientific requirements. Many of the books that have been published on design methods do not, in fact, reveal complete explanations of design and project work; but mostly techniques for guiding thoughts in specific directions in certain stages of the process.

The third generation of design research was no longer based on the theory that design is a rational, problem-solving activity. Instead, it involves *a special way of thinking* in which part of the design skill is tacit knowledge, i.e. unwritten and contextual. Bryan Lawson, in his book *How Designers Think. The design process demystified* (2008), focuses on the third generation of research on design and the designer's thoughts, both rational and irrational/intuitive, in the process of *analysis through synthesis*.

Analysis through synthesis

Designers have different working methods, but there are some common aspects in the endeavor to create new products and environments. This was shown clearly by Bryan Lawson, when he gave the same assignment to two groups of students and found that they consistently used completely different strategies to arrive at a solution. One group comprised student researchers from natural science programs and the other group comprised architecture students in their final year. The research students concentrated on analyzing the problem thoroughly to look for underlying rules. The architecture students began delivering results very quickly. Their strategy was to sidestep the initial in-depth analysis and start by testing several alternative solutions, which led to new insights and new ways to approach the problem. They worked *simultaneously* on the problem and on the solution.

Professor of design methodology Ömer Akin had previously noticed that analysis and synthesis are used concurrently, not separated, in different phases of the design process. He found that designers are continuously producing new goals and redefining boundaries. Analysis is included in all of the design phases and synthesizing starts very early.

Analyzing by synthesizing is a very apt description of the actual method that architects use—one that gives them better opportunities for handling the complexity and uncertainties than the scientist's characteristic linear process. While sketching, parts are combined into wholes, but these wholes are incomplete and unfinished, which you can see and understand when you relate them to your own interpretation of the problem. That results in new rounds of sketching, as described by Bryan Lawson:

> controlling and varying the design process is one of the most important skills a designer must develop....The designer is actually expected to contribute problems as well as solutions. Since neither finding problems nor producing solutions can be seen as predominantly logical activities we must expect the design process to demand the highest levels of creative thinking. (Lawson 2008, 124)

Bryan Lawson describes *analysis through synthesis* by explaining the activities that are involved: *formulating, representing, moving, bringing problems and solutions together, evaluating* and *reflecting*. These do not occur in any particular order; they are all woven together.

Design problems can be badly structured or ambiguous, requiring a re-formulation. *Formulating* is a way of identifying and understanding a design problem without moving logically from a problem to a solution. Focusing from several viewpoints aids in delineating boundaries, which is one of the most fundamental, and also most critical, aspects of the design process. *Representing* concerns the different ways of communicating thoughts: with drawings, models, computer simulations, text, etc. in order to engage in a dialog with the situation. This dialog is a core skill that has a great influence on the results of a design process. *Moving* represents the flow of thinking among different proposals and the creation of ideas for a solution. These ideas can be innovative or transformative, if they reinterpret existing ideas. During these movements, disordered thoughts can flow freely so that boundaries and concepts (primary generators) can be created.[4] *Bringing problems and solutions together* occurs continuously in a sort of negotiation between the two. When you formulate and test different potential solutions, your understanding of the problem increases. The ability to think on parallel tracks and to avoid concentrating too quickly on one solution seems essential. *Evaluating* means that a designer must be able to make *both* subjective and objective choices and evaluations, and also to have an idea of the advantages and disadvantages of the chosen solution, even when there are many variables that cannot be measured. A designer also has to know, just like an artist, when to finish developing a product and to end the design process. *Reflecting* means that designers need to find a balance between reflection and critical evaluation of their own opinions. The important thing is to see the key factors in different situations. The fundamental values of the profession are used, but designers often develop their own set of intellectual standpoints and conceptions, knowledge and references as a base for their reflections.

Now we have enough general knowledge to understand the thought process of designers and the characteristics of design skills, but, according to Nigel Cross (1992), we still need a comprehensive name that would help convey research findings to practicing professionals and teachers. In the early decades of design research, simplified but forceful terms were used to illustrate design in different ways: as a *problem-solving process*, an *information management process*, a *decision-making process*, or *pattern formulation*. It is clear that none of these summaries are completely wrong, since they all cover some facet of the design process. It is true that the designer does solve many problems, manages a very large amount of information, makes innumerable decisions on what to choose, and tries to understand an overriding problem by interpreting the pattern of inherent variables. However, the order of these activities is hard to comprehend and none of the definitions are really correct in the sense of capturing and successfully summarizing the *full* complexity of the design process. The definition by Lawson—*analysis through synthesis*, which he based on the latest generation of design research—

is actually a very good and adequate summary of what Nigel Cross was seeking. The concept is also apparently paradoxical enough to draw the interest of designers, practitioners and theorists.

The process of analyzing through synthesizing may be compared with a *series of qualified guesses*. You only know if the question was asked correctly after producing an answer and then checking it. The architect's typical instinctive focus on possibilities and solutions actually provides a constructive attitude toward all kinds of problems, not just architectonic ones.

Individual variation

Designers mainly use a method of analyzing a series of syntheses, but the rhythm of this process can be highly variable. The question *How do you design buildings?* was posed by architecture professor Lennart Holm to several renowned Swedish architects, among others Nils Ahrbom, Bengt Edman and Leonie Geisendorf. Nils Ahrbom, who designed a number of schools in several Swedish cities, said that he didn't want to let his co-workers start sketching until they had collected extensive knowledge about the project. He did *not* believe that:

> *you can get a vision or an idea about the entire question until you have delved deep into the problem. The genesis of an idea is the result of a compilation of knowledge relating to the specific problem.* (Holm 1990, 17)

In Ahrbom's case, synthesizing began only after one had pursued an understanding of the problem with other tactics: reading relevant literature, studying comparable projects and specifications, etc. This method has similarities to the scientific approach that the research students employed to gain understanding of a problem in Lawson's example, described earlier. Nonetheless, the sum total of knowledge does not automatically generate a design idea, so even in this case a final solution has to be selected from a number of possible ones.

Townhouses in Bagarmossen, Stockholm,
1956. Architect: Charles-Edouard and
Léonie Geisendorf. Photo: Sune Sundahl

An architect well known for his Brutalist architecture, Bengt Edman, had a different strategy. To him, order was uninteresting; the interesting part was what happened during the process. When he got a commission, he started sketching right away and continued to sketch and sketch until, as he says, someone came and took the drawings off his table—as he kept on sketching. (This must indicate that he wanted to delay the final decisions as long as possible, hoping that he might discover a better solution than the one he had.) His understanding of the problem grew in concert with his sketching, which is a search by synthesis.

Léonie Geisendorf usually got a good general idea fairly quickly, and then she would start, as she puts it, a "seduction process" to make her client comprehend how good her idea was.

Ideas for solutions pop up, are tested, rejected, and re-appear...
Then you have a vision, sometimes early, sometimes later.
I believe in that one. I don't want to analyze it to bits.
(Holm 1990, 42)

When Holm asked her if she tested other ideas, she replied in surprise: *"Can there be other ideas?"* Her working method is characterized by a strong faith in intuition. The role of intuition in sketching is illustrated by Frank Gehry's explanation of his design method. In an interview on the occasion of the presentation of a spectacular new 76-storey skyscraper in New York, he said:

Every time we start a project, we make at least 50 models. I get
an intuition, make a model that shows what I envisioned, and
get an intuitive response. I can't plan it differently, because if I
knew exactly what to do from the start, I wouldn't have to make
any models. (Rifbjerg 2011)

Beginners and experts

How can you reach the confidence in your intuition that many experienced designers talk about? Do you need to have a unique talent? Professor Nigel Cross (1990), who I mentioned earlier, approached

this question by using observations and extensive research to analyze what an experienced designer *actually does*. He listed the following aspects of a designer's work:
- produce new, unexpected solutions
- tolerate uncertainties and work with incomplete information
- apply imagination and constructive foresight to practical problems
- use different media: drawings and models as tools for problem-solving

To achieve these tasks, designers need the following skills/talents (Cross 1992):
- they must be able to recognize and re-formulate poorly defined problems
- use strategies based on tentative solutions
- be able to change goals and constraints and exercise this freedom as they design
- use "abductive" thinking, i.e. allow an understanding to grow gradually by alternating between theory and empirical studies
- use both creative and critical thinking
- be able to use non-verbal, graphic and three-dimensional modeling media

The aspect that received a great deal of interest from Cross was the difference between how experienced designers worked compared to beginners. His comparisons of students from the lower versus higher levels of industrial design educations showed that they had different strategies for gathering information and knowledge while working on a design project. You would expect that the beginners would have much more difficulty, but that was not the case. In fact, they did not gather much information and they would examine the problem and solve it as something simple, without being aware that additional priorities could be applied. Among the older students, you could discern two groups. One group presented creative solutions of high quality. They didn't ask too many questions or research too much, but they continuously processed what they did know and gave the impression of constantly evaluating the problem by testing various solutions. They searched for priorities and chose them fairly early in the process. The students in the other group collected a lot of information, but sometimes this research appeared to be a substitute for the actual design work. Their efforts did not produce different variations of possible solutions.[5]

Many studies confirm that experienced "expert designers" focus on the solution instead of the problem. The fact that the beginners in the previous example considered it a simple problem and didn't seek alternative solutions can indicate that the ability to *analyze through synthesis* develops during their education, as they gain experience from multiple design attempts. The question is then: Why were there still older students who did not fully utilize the analysis–synthesis method? It may possibly depend on the following factors:
- They did not understand the method and concealed their insecurity by gathering excessive information.
- They were too self-critical and rejected all their solutions as deficient even before trying to consolidate and review them.
- They did not dare develop their visions because they felt unable to succeed because of their lack of ability and insufficient knowledge, or they were unsure if their idea was "right" or "in fashion".

An inhibiting insecurity is part of each of these possible explanations. Assisting students to conquer such fear requires individual, insightful guidance that helps them to be courageous and *dare to make mistakes*. They can learn a lot more by doing that than by nervously avoiding any setbacks. This means that architectural education should focus a great deal of attention on the design process and not solely, which is often the case, on the product and its representation, i.e. the presented proposal.

Stadelhofen Railway Station, Zürich, Switzerland 1983–1984.
Canopy of steel frames and glass, shaped like a cupped hand.
Architect: Santiago Calatrava. Photo: Jesús Azpeita Seron

An extensive overview of research and the interviews by Cross with successful designers reveal that the strategy used by beginners may be called an in-depth focus, which means that they often immediately identify *one* aspect of the problem, formulate *one* solution and investigate this in depth. This results in partial solutions that may be difficult to combine into a satisfying final solution. Experienced designers will often start with a wide and open overview of the problem and then begin developing concurrent and relevant solutions that resemble quick guesses. They then use these guesses, based on their prior experience, to explore and define the problem and its solution simultaneously. Accomplished designers *do not* start with a comprehensive analysis of the problem; they apply *analysis through synthesis*. They constrain the problem and reshape it, if necessary, based on the ideas that are generated and self-criticized in the sketching process.

It can often take a long time for beginners to reach the confidence of a professional. The development can span far beyond the school years. Lawson and Dorst refer to a model developed by philosophy professor Hubert Dreyfus, who wrote about the following six steps in a designer's development: *a novice, an advanced beginner, a competent problem-solver, the expert, the master and the visionary.* A self-evaluation that is done periodically in the Industrial Design Department at The Eindhoven University of Technology shows that their review of their own development coincided with the first three steps of the model. Several of the Eindhoven students felt that they had reached the level of *a competent problem-solver*, which is characterized by the following:

> *Problem solving at this level involves the seeking of opportunities. The process takes on a trial-and-error character, with some learning and reflection. A problem solver that goes on to be proficient, immediately sees the most important issues and appropriate plan, and then reasons out what to do.*
> (Lawson and Dorst 2009, 98–101)

Notes

1 Adrian Forty (2004, 137) cites the following formulation in a translation of Alberti's De Re Aedificatoria, published in 1726: "The whole art of building consists in the design, and in the structure."
2 Rosell 1990, 17.
3 Schön 1990 (1986), 100.
4 The notions of concept and primary generator, etc. are covered in Chapter 6.
5 Cross (2004, 429) cites Christiaan and Dorst's 1992 protocol evaluation.

References

Akin, Ömer: *Psychology of Architectural Design*. London, Pion Limited 1986

Björkman, Armand: *Skisser och sånt*. Arkitektur Förlag 1988, 9

Cross, Nigel: *The Nature and Nurture of Design Ability*. Design Studies, Vol. 11, No. 3, July 1990, 130

Cross, Nigel: *On Design Ability*. In: Kazemian, A. Reza: *Proceedings. International Conference on Theories and Methods of Design*. The Royal Institute of Technology, School of Architecture 1992, 47–56

Cross, Nigel: *Expertise in Design: An Overview*. Design Studies, Vol. 25, No. 5, 2004, 429

Cross, Nigel: *Design Thinking. Understanding How Designers Think and Work*. Berg, Oxford 2011, 29, 144–146

Forty, Adrian: *Words and Buildings. A Vocabulary of Modern Architecture*. Thames & Hudson 2004 (2000), 136–138

Holm, Lennart: *Att rita hus*. Arkitekturförlag, Stockholm 1990

Lawson, Bryan: *How Designers Think. The Design Process Demystified*. Architectural Press 2008, 3, 33–50,

123–126, 289–301

Lawson, Bryan; Dorst, Kees:
Design Expertise. Routledge 2009,
98–101

Lundeqvist, Jerker: *Design och produkt-*
utveckling. Metoder och begrepp.
Studentlitteratur 1995, 61–77

Moholy-Nagy, L.: *Vision in Motion.*
2nd printing. Paul Theobald,
Chicago 1947, 42

Olsson, Sölve: *Om gestaltningsprocessen.*
Tidskrift för Arkitekturforskning,
Vol. 2, No. 1–2, 1989, 95–99

Rifbjerg, Synne: Weekendavisen (Dk)
October 14, 2011

Rosell, Gustaf: *Anteckningar om design-*
processen. Kungliga Tekniska
Högskolan 1990, 17

Schön, Donald A.: *Educating the*
Reflective Practitioner. Toward
a New Design for Teaching and
Learning in the Professions.
Jossey-Bass Publishers,
San Francisco 1990 (1986), 100

Vial, Stéphane: *Kort avhandling om*
design. Dolhem Förlag 2011, 24–26

Wolf, Gary: *Steve Jobs: The Next*
Insanely Great Thing. Wired 1996.
http://www.wired.com/wired/
archive/4.02/jobs_pr.html

6 Analysis through synthesis
—in practice

Formulating the problems

Identifying a problem, formulating and interpreting it, is critical to the results of design work. The meaning of the term "*problem*" as used here is the task description, including specific aspects or perspectives. The word *problem* is somewhat of an obstacle in a discussion, because "problems and problem-solving" are concepts that are considered to be connected in a linear sequence. When you have a problem, you look for a solution; unsolved problems cause discomfort. On the other hand, research shows that design is not only a question of problem-solving. There are always different ways to look at design problems, because they are multi-dimensional and the solutions may be used for different purposes. This complexity, however, contains both traps and uncertainties.

Design problems are generally ambiguous and unstructured, which are two of the greatest obstacles to introducing rational methods for design. The client's formulation and initial conception of a design problem can be faulty and this may require a few steps forward and back in the design process to rectify. Nonetheless, sensitivity to the client's opinion is fundamental; anything else would display arrogance. The architect can then use his or her professional skill to discuss other interpretations of the problem that the client may be unaware of. Thus the way the architect interprets the problem can be a teaching opportunity.

An example of reinterpretation of a problem was a thesis project for a winery and wine cellar on the island of Öland. According to the original formulation, the winery was to be seen as a workplace for production, indicating an emphasis on work conditions and production logistics. However, the thesis candidate realized that there would be advantages to looking at it as a year-round tourist destination. Not only would there be additional jobs, but also a chance to utilize the extensive infrastructure that already served the summer tourists. This new problem formulation influenced the brief and the subsequent design.

The process of orienting oneself in the problem/solution world and testing tentative syntheses is continuous (not just an initial task which you don't have to return to). You need the ability to develop parallel paths for thinking that *allow ambiguity and uncertainty*. Making choices prematurely can limit the possibilities for finding good solutions.

Experienced designers start with a wide overview of the problem. They can advance from the details to the holistic level or, in reverse, from the whole to the individual details. These movements are often like a *pendulum*. A designer can move from sketching a stair handrail to an overview of fire safety issues, or from designing a library to an in-depth study of library and information science. The latter can turn into a trap which is very common in thesis projects, namely that a candidate can become overly captivated by a large new field of studies and thus lose focus on the project formulation. For example, a student can present their new, detailed knowledge of liturgy, without successfully applying the results to their proposal for a well-planned church building. This can happen because of uncertainty in deciding which interpretation of the problem is relevant, but it can also be a way of avoiding the risk of making incorrect choices and exposing a lack of knowledge when you convert your own (sometimes vague) perceptions and imaginary pictures into physical forms.

Deciding at what point to finish the design work is part of the actual definition of the design problem, i.e. which aspects it is necessary to be aware of. In other words, there is no clear end to the design process. A designer must decide, just like an artist, when to stop the process. Knowing when is a matter of skill and proficiency.

That is why less experienced architects can have difficulties completing work on time.

An important part of the design problem may be present in something that already exists. Defining such a problem entails decisions on which parts to incorporate. According to Professor of Theory and History of Design Jan Michl, the concept of design tends to be seen as a solitary act, but in fact it always has cumulative and collective dimensions. Designers always build on, modify and continue what other designers have created. *Redesign* is a more accurate concept, and should be used more often, especially in design education, because it broadens the design perspective, he says. You can also look at Michl's idea in a wider perspective, namely of formulating your own interpretation by critically inspecting another designer's evaluation of the problem.

Architects strive for originality in their buildings and environments. It is rare that you hear someone like the Swedish architect Gert Wingårdh speaking so openly in an interview about starting a project by reworking other architects' projects:

> *– I never put myself in the situation of starting with a blank sheet of paper. If I'm going to design a hotel, I get out other drawings of hotels and begin altering them. I change them and change them and finally I get something entirely new. That way I get into a flow in the work and I know the result will be good.*
> *–Isn't that cheating? A risk of plagiarism?*
> *–To copy a drawing is plagiarism, of course. But I never do that.*

(Magazine Skiss, No. 4, 1990)

Architect Peter Zumthor talks about a similar insight:

> *Design is inventing. When I was still at arts and crafts school, we tried to follow this principle. We looked for a new solution to every problem. We felt it was important to be avant-garde. Not until later did I realize that there are basically only a very few architectural problems for which a valid solution has not already been found.* (Zumthor 1998, 21)

Demarcation of boundaries, dichotomy games and alternating

The process of surveying the complexity of a problem and discerning the important features, in order to be able to start a design, is characterized by a sequence of episodes, as described by architecture professor Peter G. Rowe. He states that in these episodes, the following things can happen: (1) Intellectual movement back and forth between fields of interest that can include both the architectural form and evaluation of the brief, to structures and other technical aspects. (2) Periods of unbridled speculation, followed by periods of contemplation, when the designer "takes stock of the situation". (3) *Organizing principles,* which are independent, are involved in each episode; a dialogue between the designer and the situation is established. (4) The episodic character of the process subsides as the problem becomes more well defined and contained.

You can get a deeper understanding of a problem by looking at it from different perspectives, i.e. by stepping away and looking at it from the *outside*. Various methods may be used for these individual shifts of perspective, including the use of viewpoints contributed by different people (brainstorming). But you can also look from *inside* the problem *out* at the surrounding situation. By sketching, you can then examine what limits there are and what is possible. Finding and demarcating boundaries speeds up the design process. How far can I go before losing the important aspects? What really *are* the important aspects? What is unthinkable? What is possible?

Architects define their range of motion, not by placing boundaries around a problem like a fence, but by the opposite approach of investigating how far they *can* go, what obstacles there are, and what potential opportunities there may be. In this discussion of boundaries, it would be generally true to say that architects do not concentrate on what they *cannot do*, but rather on *what they can do*. To succeed, he or she has to make continuous, sometimes apparently unbounded, thought movements.

Most of us know how a perspective changes as we ride a swing.

The world looks different from above and from below, and then there are all the sensations of movement. Sometimes you either want or need to slow down by braking moderately or in desperation. You have to be constantly prepared to adjust to gravity as needed, on one side or the other. To a large extent, working as an architect involves having a comparable flexible preparedness for the swings of thought and the alternation between the conflicting requirements of the task and the need to reach an optimal solution. The alternating movement helps in showing where the boundaries are and simultaneously provides opportunities to see the problem from a new viewpoint. Like the limits of a pendulum swing, opposing pairs of concepts, or *dichotomies*, are used when architects try to understand problems and determine the maximum range of possible solutions. The conceptual pairs can be sensory, and related to what you can see, hear, touch, etc. They can also be connected to three-dimensional spatial perception or be taken from the world of geometry or technology. Commonly used dichotomies are: light–dark, big–little, light–heavy, horizontal–vertical, hard–soft, over–under, mass–void.

As an example of this, in a Danish architectural competition for developing ideas for new suburbs, the participants were asked to explicitly or implicitly relate to overall urban, functional, sociocultural, mentally semantic and ecological aspects by utilizing 30 dichotomies. Among these were the commonly used ones:
high–low, heavy–light, tight–dispersed, static–dynamic, permanent–temporary, real–imaginary,
but also the conceptual pairs that steered the issues of suburban development—everyday dichotomies like:
order–freedom, local–global, collective–individual, meaningful–meaningless, presence–absence, among others.
(Aarhus 2001).

Different dichotomies can clarify sensual qualities that are considered to be abstract, or place focus on technical and practical aspects. This can lead to new associations and more space for feasible solutions. *Light/dark* can thus express the symbolism of illumination, personal memories of light, the experiential preferences of others, and eyes squinting, and even technical aspects. It can also remind us of the Japanese author Tanizaki's poetic love of shadows and lead us into reflections on darkness. Perceptions about sensual, very material, tactile qualities and colors can be interspersed with abstract thoughts on spatial geometry or ruminations on construction and sustainability, economy and usability. There is no given order for these reflections; one thought can spark another unexpectedly. The result is that a designer can discover that the criteria and brief formulated by a client may need to be revised and opened up for new ideas and a different solution than what had seemed likely in the beginning.

Dichotomy games and alternating between different levels in design help create a sensual and rational connection to your own project and they also help define the situation in relation to the peripheral boundaries. They can also give you a sense of being physically present in the proposal that you are working on. This extended vision can provide new associations and inspiration for new interpretations of site conditions, activities, exterior spaces, different materials, etc. The dichotomy game can be playful when you are amused by discovering improbable things, or by the satisfaction of suddenly seeing the obvious. Alternating between dichotomies or between situations that appear incompatible, thinking in metaphors and formulating paradoxes characterize several aspects of the architect's work and the architect's way of thinking.

The primary generator, the guiding principle, the concept

Extricating a specific attribute or quality to use for understanding the assigned problem can reveal the path to the solution. The nature of the specific attribute can vary from case to case. It can be special terrain conditions, the character and color of the landscape, or perhaps the client's dreams, the type of activity, production processes, etc. Both practical and technical as well as poetic metaphors may be applicable, depending on the character of the problem. A well-known example from Sweden in the 1980s was when architect Bengt Lindroos humorously admitted that the design inspiration for his winning entry in the architectural competition for new buildings at Slussen in central Stockholm was a cheddar cheese.

This specific attribute or quality that you are searching for can be expressed in different terms. Peter G. Rowe calls these strong aspects *organizing principles* and he sees them as a model that steers decisions during the design process. Bryan Lawson calls them *guiding principles* which suggests sensitivity and the security of being guided. Jane Darke then introduced the concept of *the primary generator* for these aspects. Her term is especially appropriate because it connotes a dynamic force that drives the project forward. Another nearly synonymous term was coined by the Swedish architects Tham & Videgård: *architectonically active elements*, which they say they look for each time they initiate a new project.[1]

In some countries, the term *concept* is used for nascent ideas like this. Certainly, the interest for conceptual art that developed at the end of the 1960s contributed to its popularity as an architectural term. The basic thought was that the idea, or concept, predominates over the material or aesthetic considerations. The word *concept* comes from the identical Latin word and the related *concipio,* which refers not just to an idea, but also to an embryo, vessel or reservoir. An idea is an abstraction while *a concept* also includes purpose (goal), form and materiality.

In the field of science, it is essential that the terminology is explicit and unequivocal. But design is not a science, since subjective values and imagination combine with objective values. Perhaps the terms used do not have to be completely precise and distinct, and even if there are slight differences in their meanings, they describe the designer's initial thought process and may be used in the professional discourse. As a student or educated architect you can choose the term that best stimulates thoughts, liberates the perception, and supports your work.

Formulating an overall idea (including recognizing its inherent consequences) to help interpret a problem can be a risky undertaking, because what you choose is of great importance to the whole design process and the finalized solution. Sometimes the key aspect is immediately apparent, even if it may be less important at later stages. The question to be asked when formulating the concept is: *What is important/specific?* This often takes time to clarify. Meanwhile, the designer can accumulate knowledge through case studies, research, etc. There can be several aspects that vie for attention. The uncertainty of knowing if you have made the right choices or if you have enough knowledge to handle them can be paralyzing. To understand the situation, you sketch tentative solutions, test them against external criteria or your own, and return to the problem to see which primary generator or guiding principle has the best chance of driving the work forward. This should be done relatively early, after you have tested a few tentative solutions and have understood how to view the problem. However, if you realize after deeper study that the original idea is inappropriate, you have to reject it and find another one. In other words, *kill your darlings*. If you are already far into the process, this may indicate that the qualified guess you made in choosing the overall idea was not quite professionally chosen.

This groundwork supports the design process, giving it a clear direction, which delineates the character of the proposal. At the same time, you find out what knowledge you may need to seek and develop. This is very individual. Occasionally the important factors are obvious; what the architectonically active elements are, or the organizing principles, but it often takes time to find the right "entry" and this can be frustrating. This search requires receptivity to any impressions. It is often a good idea to take the most obvious choice to get the process started; to take a first step toward understanding conditions and limits. Therefore, it is inappropriate to have too many restrictions at the start of the design process because they inhibit and reduce the range of possible interpretations and resulting solutions. But latching on tenaciously to an early concept can be problematic, too. Designers sometimes hang on doggedly to their concepts. Design students can often create more problems than they solve by choosing impractical concepts which generate additional problems.

A telling example can be a thesis project focusing on the design of an elementary school. The proposal was based in a municipality that suggested an appropriate site for the school. The site was part of a park that was adjacent to a ravine. At the bottom of the ravine there was an industrial lot, affected by heavy truck traffic. The student became frustrated because she had decided that the park and its character had to be preserved at any cost, but she quickly realized that it would be very difficult. The school building and its entry roads covered a large area, and many of the placements of the buildings that she considered chopped the site into small chunks. She held on to her concept and rejected many sketches, but finally everything fell into place when she situated the school building on the lot boundary by the ravine. It also became known that you could get a variance from the municipality's site plan, which actually disallowed buildings on the lot boundary. The park was kept more or less intact and the proposed placement solved other problems: access roads and interior circulation could be well planned, the design of the building took on a powerful form and expression, and the building itself provided an important buffer against the ravine and the industrial lot.

An overall idea is used as an important motor in the design process, but it may also be utilized later to define or create a special atmosphere around a building. Daniel Libeskind was criticized for using widely different conceptual explanations for identical architectonic elements. First, he described the characteristic slices in the facade of the Jewish Museum in Berlin as an expression for the thriving businesses of the Jewish community in that area prior to the Nazi takeover. It was therefore surprising that he had a different explanation when he used the same facade treatment for the Royal Ontario Museum in Toronto: the slices were points of crystal. Their main function was to indicate public space for participation, interaction and dance (Silber 2007).

Sensory memories and the architect's experience can be important in the quest for the character of a proposal. For example, Peter Zumthor likes to start with childhood memories to awaken the sensory experiences that give him the feeling of intense presence:

> Looking back, it seems as if this was the only room in the house in which the ceiling did not disappear into twilight; the small hexagonal tiles on the floor, dark red and fitted so tightly together that the cracks between them were almost imperceptible, were hard and unyielding under my feet, and the smell of oil paint issued from the kitchen cupboard. Everything about this kitchen was typical of a traditional kitchen. There was nothing special about it. But perhaps it was just the fact that it was so very much, so very naturally, a kitchen that has imprinted its memory indelibly on my mind. The atmosphere of this room is insolubly linked with my idea of a kitchen. (Zumthor 1998, 9)

Zumthor is not the only prominent architect who considers their childhood spatial experiences a well of sensibility for their artistic endeavors. Luis Barragán retrieved colors for the famous San Cristóbal Estates in Mexico City from the houses and soil in the little Mexican village where he grew up.[2] And for the Danish architect Henning Larsen, the special light that he saw in his childhood church was a source of inspiration throughout his life (Møller 2000). In the case of Eva Jiricna, well known for designing probably the world's first high-tech glass stair, the issue was an interest in and sensitivity for material expression:

> We always try to limit the amount of materials on each scheme…. So the material is a very early decision. I think that in a way material dictates the concept…you can only interpret certain concepts with certain materials because materials are not inter-changeable. In terms of space it depends on whether you clad with say aluminium panels, or fibrous plaster or just paint the walls. The material really is the starting point of the story and use of the material somehow helps to put together a concept.

(Eva Jiricna quoted in Lawson and Dorst 2009, 179)

The choice of a concept is, as the above example illustrates, strongly colored by the designer's experiences and observations, but also by his or her individual interests and values (see Chapter 10). The choice is further influenced by the sensitive dialog you have with the situation during the sketching periods.

Sketching and searching

Sketches, drawings, construction documents, models, various data and text that are used in design *represent* the future products. There are two main types of representation: one type works *inward* so that designers can communicate with their own thoughts and perceptions. It is a kind of dialog between the designer and his or her evaluation of the problem and the situation. The other type of representation is directed *outward* and includes the presentation materials and working drawings used to present the proposal to teachers, colleagues, clients, consultants, builders, etc.

In architectural education you mainly come into contact with sketches and presentation drawings. *Sketching*, and the specific searching that sketching involves, deserves special recognition, because it is one of the foundations of the design method. The other foundation is criticism of your work—both self-criticism and from others—which is necessary for dealing with complex design problems.[3]

The word "sketch" is most often used according to its Italian root *schisso*, which denotes a summarizing draft or a preliminary study for the final formulation of a graphic composition, thought, etc. A sketch can also be a way of taking notes; for instance, a travel sketch. But the most important kinds of sketches are the ones used to investigate the problems you are grappling with, while searching for a solution. *The soul of the sketch is the search*[4]—a fundamental part of the architect's working method. These sketches are used to extract inner images that may be judged and considered as possible solutions to the problem. Architecture actually happens in the mind of the architect. Sketches release visions. They don't have to be beauti-

Above: The stair at Joseph Sloane Street, London (no longer existing), probably the world's first high-tech glass stair. Design: Eva Jiricna, 1989. One flight of the stair was later installed in the Christensen Shop in Copenhagen.

Opposite: The detail of the stair at Boodles, Liverpool, UK. A spiral glass staircase forms a link between the old and the new elements of the shop.

ful or legible for anyone other than the designer.

Sketching and the process of sketching are essential to the formulation of tentative and final solutions. Paradoxically, this special sketch technique includes both a wide, relaxed overview and a *simultaneous* sharp concentration of thought. This activity covers all the "latent possibilities for action" that exist in the environment; those that can be measured objectively and also those that are related to the designer and therefore dependent on his or her ability.[5] Precisely this ability to discover latent possibilities is indicative of the architect's professional skill. In this work, both the intellect and the senses are active and cooperating. The inspiration you seek when you are formulating or re-formulating a problem and choosing a concept can come from visual, audio-visual, or tactile associations. The senses can be a source, but sensory impressions are controlled by experience and knowledge. This exact, or at least disciplined, form of sensual imagination is necessary in a few professions, one of them being architecture.[6]

When you start a new project, the freedom to choose from many possible solutions can be paralyzing. The choice of a concept or "architectonically active elements" gives a direction, but you still need some sort of limit, either self-imposed or assigned. *Sketching* is actually a veiled term for investigating the range of possibilities by identifying boundaries, both physical and psychological, while searching for an overall direction. Metaphors and dichotomies are used at this stage as tools to create objective distance or control.

The most intense thought dynamics occur during the initial sketching phase when irrevocable decisions are made concerning the direction and design of a proposal. This is often a very time-consuming thought process that, incidentally, is rarely recognized by clients (but can be reflected in the relative charges for different stages of design work). The first phase of design contains the majority of the creative work: identifying the main features of the problem and, if necessary, re-formulating it convincingly. *Sketching is a tool for analyzing through synthesizing.* This involves a specific way of thinking and working and the *courage to choose*, which is based on rational decision-making and also professional skill, including subjective values. Making models and drawings as sketches that are abstract or sensual, serious or frivolous, focused on the assignment or reaching for external inspiration, introduces questions that a designer would not have asked otherwise. Thoughts mature in this process, so they can be more easily articulated in discussions with co-workers or teachers at an architecture school. After additional development, the proposal may be presented to a client or critics.

> *A designer who cannot sketch is likely not to be able to "converse"*
> *freely with the situation. Drawings are undoubtedly amongst*
> *the most central and important of all these representations.*
> Lawson (2008, 293)

But he adds that it appears that a designer's key skill is not necessarily the ability to create a great variety of representations, but the ability to discriminate between them to get an appropriate understanding of the problem.

With the aid of sketches, the architect can weigh different possible concepts, formulate syntheses, and choose promising solutions, while others are rejected. The designer can be misled by wishful thinking through their initial conceptions. It is only when the first inner images are committed to paper or when a digital or physical model is produced that you can clearly see the pros and cons of the proposed solution. It is then possible to critically review and evaluate the mutual dependence between the problem and the solution and their consequences. In that sense, it is proper training for dealing with the complexity of architectural work. The ability to draw is not essential, since you can actually sketch with other tools. For example, Kazuyo Sejima[7] doesn't primarily do freehand sketches. Instead she prefers to sketch by making a large number of physical models in various scales. This has not prevented her from renewing architectural thought and reaching world renown in the process.

Sketches, of all kinds, are notes showing the development of thoughts. You must be comfortable with the chosen representation technique in order to use its specific rhythm in a relaxed way. Thoughts should be allowed to flow freely. You may need time to notice possible openings—or obstacles that you can trip over. They can actually be important sources of inspiration. In a discussion about architectural education, some Swiss teachers noted that "positive naiveté" and mistakes can be used constructively in design work (Angélil and Hebel 2008). But this requires that you help the students tame their own self-criticism. It is an important observation that mistakes and naiveté can open your eyes to new possibilities. It doesn't make a lot of difference how you sketch, as long as you use the technique you're comfortable with, but it is necessary *that* you sketch in order to develop your thoughts and search for new knowledge. However, for the sake of clarity it may be added that in the end you are dealing with a *professionally qualified guess*, which is, at one and the same time, the constant anxiety-inducing and satisfying challenge of creative design work.

The range of individual sketch techniques is broad. This is apparent when you study work methods that are applied at some of the world's leading architectural offices. For example, Steven Holl uses watercolors to get an initial grasp of the atmosphere and feeling he wants to capture. At SANAA and at OMA they start, to a large extent, from brainstorming around physical models that are developed by a project group as alternative syntheses. The advantage of physical models compared to digital presentations, for example, is that you can see the whole, and the variations of the building form at the same time. Several people can also gather around a physical model, and both the lead architect's and trainee's viewpoints can be equally important, when everyone is looking at the same object. On the other hand, at Jean Nouvel's architectural office, physical models are considered to be too abstract as representations. Nouvel prefers verbal formulations. His thesis project was apparently written, not drawn, which is rare for architectural thesis projects.[8] Santiago Calatrava often starts his work, as mentioned earlier, by drawing an

New Museum of Contemporary Art, New York City 2007.
Architect: Kazuyo Sejima + Ryue Nishizawa / SANAA.
Photo: Dean Kaufman

Rolex Learning Center (the campus hub and library) for EPFL
(Ecole Polytechnique Federale de Lausanne), Switzerland 2010.
Architect: Kazuyo Sejima + Ryue Nishizawa / SANAA.
Photo: SANAA

analysis of kinetic forces in the human body: for example, a hand in movement, and then converting these studies into advanced structures like the bridges in Sevilla and Bilbao. Frank Gehry, as quoted previously, searches through piles of models or sketches for the form that corresponds to his intuitive inner vision. In the Bilbao Guggenheim audio guide Gehry says that he consciously avoided thinking when he started sketching the museum. He drew blurry figures, completely without intellectual guidance and without any intention, until he arrived at the museum's spectacular form. Some of these sketches, which resemble totally inaccessible doodles, are reproduced in the museum publications.

Using a sketching technique that you're not comfortable with can be inhibiting. This was the case, for example, with a student who had great difficulty formulating her proposal when she did pencil sketches. She thought she was expected to do it that way, but her work was constrained and frustration set in. When it was discovered that she was very skilled at watercolors she started using that technique instead, and the change was immediate. She could access her own thoughts and eventually present them to others.

The importance of the work of the hand as an extension of the mind in sketching is described by Martin Heidegger:

> *Every motion of the hand in every one of its works carries itself through the element of thinking, every bearing of the hand bears itself in that element. All the work of the hand is rooted in thinking.* (Heidegger 1993, 381)

Digital modeling now often competes with the traditional artistic, manual techniques such as sculpture, drawing and painting. The discipline that a computer demands differs from other artistic techniques in that the computer program defines the possibilities. The extent to which it allows completely free association depends on the architect's or designer's individual approach and ability. One of the advantages of computer modeling is that you can quickly test different forms from different viewpoints and perspectives and, if necessary, be able to change them in different ways. Those students who don't have enough confidence in their own ability in freehand drawing or painting can avoid being inhibited by using computers.

Furthermore, the rapid and constant developments in digital technology are likely to bring forth opportunities that we cannot imagine today. However, there can be a disparity in how different generations relate to analog versus digital culture and occasionally there may be knowledge gaps between students and their teachers concerning familiarity with computers. There are also doubts and mixed opinions about to what extent digital techniques give as much freedom for association and a relaxed relationship to thought, as does hand sketching. Will it be possible to do digital sketches that are as free and without conscious intent—while the inner visions have time to mature—as the ones done by Frank Gehry?

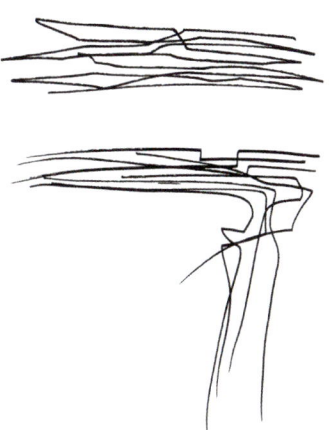

Above: Interior of the MAXXI Museum, Rome, 2009. Architect: Zaha Hadid. A circulation pattern of hanging pathways connects the museum's interior to its urban context. Photo: Roland Halbe Architekturfotografie

Left: A conceptual sketch by Zaha Hadid showing the first ideas for movement through the MAXXI Museum. Zaha Hadid Architects

A Summer Reflection

It is clear that Nobel Prize winner Saul Bellow has succeeded with the seemingly impossible, namely to capture thoughts in all their disorder and erratic movement. In Humboldt's Gift, *his tool is the special storytelling technique, which is even more prominent in* Herzog, *perhaps the most famous of his books. In* Herzog, *the narrator wanders through different life events, weaving in "letters" now and then: brief pieces that he writes in his mind to various people, short or long texts in the moment, sometimes to the woman he loves, sometimes to a person in power or to an enemy. Just as when you converse and comment in your thoughts; when you openly and without censorship mix emotions with logic, fuzziness with rationality, in order to finally distill the complexity into an explicit formulation that matches the needs of the moment.*

What seems similar between Bellow's method of writing Herzog *and the architect's sketching is, first, the way of including notes taken "on the fly", and second, that the initial blurriness enriches the inner dialog. Subconsciously gathered experiences and images, with sensory meaning and spatial enclosure, leave their imprints in sketches. Lines and smudges express a multitude of both fragmentary and complete thoughts. If you succeed, this effort results not in a reduction, but in an accurate consolidation of the project's complexity.*

The recollections and perceptions of spaces that we store in our memory are rarely collected consciously; they are noted on the periphery as we pass by, which is indicated by the following example. A few years ago the students in the first year (about 75 people) were given an assignment in their Architectural History course that involved gathering historical materials on several buildings on a street, interviewing residents, and researching literature; all for the purpose of bringing the history of the buildings to life. Every group had one building assigned to them and on the first day everyone was nervous to see if they would actually succeed with the often difficult task of getting access to their buildings. Eventually the student work resulted in an illustrated story about the buildings, including a summary of the entire material, which was required in the assignment.

The exercise was led at the Royal Institute of Technology in Stockholm by the university lecturer in Architectural History at the time, Fredrik Bedoire. I was the head teacher for the first-year students, with responsibility for all the projects and for coordinating the subjects. I saw this work partly as an exercise in composition, where an investigation of spatial perception and spatial design was the main objective of the school year. To reinforce this goal, I supplemented the Architectural History project with an hour-long sketch exercise which I handed out to the students the day after their first visit to their assigned buildings. The assignment was as follows: "Draw your recollection of the streetscape (preferably with the building you are working on) as simple light and dark fields, contours, or any other way you remember it. You don't have to show details, just relative scale."

A sigh of protest went through the lecture hall: "I can't do it, impossible; we didn't look at the streetscape, we looked at the assigned buildings!" So I said (severely): "Deadline in one hour."

As soon as the sketch was turned in, Exercise Part 2 was handed out: "Draw the streetscape from the same point, but this time, at the real site. Make notes on the shapes and voids that are characteristic of that urban space. Think in terms of the elements that shape the urban environment: light, color, texture, etc."

At the review that afternoon, the two drawings were hung next to each other, and it was readily apparent that the first drawing, not consciously memorized, had succeeded in capturing the spatial characteristics of the streetscape, as confirmed by the second drawing.

We assigned that hour-long sketch for a couple of years, and then the element of surprise was lost. But even the students who had missed the assignment and had done replacement exercises in completely different locations could verify with their sketches that they had clear images of the space without being aware of it; they had made peripheral observations in passing, mental notes while walking to school or to the café, which they added to their reference library of architectonic spaces. I think most people do this.

We complete different tasks when we transport ourselves from one place to another. But simultaneously, in passing, we collect a treasure of spatial perceptions which we mix with our organized and disorganized thoughts. All the fundamental concepts—light/dark, hard/soft, open/closed, and direction, space and enclosure—are included.

No media has yet successfully given us the sensation of spatial enclosure. This becomes obvious when you experience environments that you have seen many times in photos or on film, in magazines or in lectures. For example, the Forbidden City is seemingly described in such detail in Bernardo Bertolucci's film The Last Emperor, *but you still experience the real place with an entirely different spatial perception. The difference lies in the feeling of enclosure, indicated by relationships like in front, behind, underneath, beside, up and down, etc. while all the senses participate in concert to read the space.*

During field studies we make conscious observations, but all the material that we gather in passing, without consciously registering it: Where is that? Can you start a dialog with the inner, latent, sensory-based spatial images? They have the advantage of being holistic (just as the periphery is as important as focusing on the core assignment) —precisely as in Herzog's constant dialogue with himself and with his surroundings.

Notes

References

1 Lauri 2009, 8–9 ("the active elements of architecture").

2 Barragán, cited in Frampton 1983, 152.

3 The roll of criticism in architectural education is covered in detail in Chapter 7.

4 Ewehag 1986, 17.

5 This activity is similar to the perception psychologist James J. Gibson's theory of affordance. (Gibson 1969, 36–42).

6 Pérez-Gómez (2006, 19) refers to Giordano Bruno's concept that the few professions which require disciplined sensual imagination are poetry, art and architecture.

7 Partner in "Kazuyo Sejima + Ryue Nishizawa / SANAA".

8 Even Gropius probably preferred to formulate himself verbally, because according to Ahnefeldt-Mollerup (2010, 255), his successful marketing of the Bauhaus ideas concealed the fact that he lacked drawing skills.

Aarhus School of Architecture: *Suburb Research Project.* 2001

Ahnefeldt-Mollerup, Merete: *Modernismen i Tyskland.* In: Caldenby, Claes; Nygaard, Erik: *Arkitekturteoriernas historia.* Forskningsrådet Formas 2010, 255

Angélil, Marc; Hebel, Dirk: *Deviations: Designing Architecture > A Manual.* Birkhäuser Verlag AB 2008

Bellow, S.: *Herzog.* Penguin Books, London 1964

Bellow, S.: *Humboldt´s Gift.* Penguin Books, London 1976

Caldenby, Claes; Nygaard, Erik: *Arkitekturteoriernas historia.* Forskningsrådet Formas 2010

Darke, Jane: *The Primary Generator and the Design Process.* Design Studies, Vol.1, No.1, 1979

Ewehag, Hans-Peter: *Skissen som arbetsmetod.* Examensarbete i visualiseringsteknik, CTH 1986

Frampton, Kenneth: *Prospects for a Critical Regionalism.* Perspecta: The Yale Architectural Journal, Vol. 20, 1983, 147–162

Gibson, James J.: *The Ecological Approach to Visual Perception.* Cornell University. Houghton Mifflin Company 1979, pp. 36-42.

Heidegger, Martin: *Basic Writings from "Being and Time" (1927) to "The Task of Thinking" (1964).* Routledge, London 1993, 381

Lauri, Tomas (ed.) with contributions by Kieran Long (AR) and Hans Ibelings (A10): *Tham & Videgård arkitekter.* Arvinius Förlag, Sweden 2009

Lawson, Bryan: *How Designers Think. The Design Process Demystified* (fourth ed). Architectural Press 2008, 4, 55–73, 293

Lawson, Bryan; Dorst, Kees: *Design Expertis.* Routledge 2009, 179

Lindroos, Bengt: Kv Ormen & Ormsaltaren, Stockholm. Arkitektur 4/1982, 14 *Magazine Skiss,* No. 4, 1990. Interview with Gert Wingårdh

Michl, Jan: *On Seeing Design as Redesign. An Exploration of a Neglected Problem in Design Education.* Scandinavian Journal of Design History, Vol 12, 2002: 7–23

Møller, Henrik Sten: *Legen og lyset.* Politiken Forlag 2000

Ockman, Joan (ed.): *Architecture School. Three Centuries of Educating Architects in North America.* MIT Press 2012

Pérez-Gómez, Alberto: *Built upon Love. Architectural Longing After Ethics and Aesthetics.* The MIT Press, Cambridge, Massachusetts Institute of Technology 2006, 19

Rowe, Peter G.: *Design Thinking.* The MIT Press, Cambridge, Massachusetts Institute of Technology 1991 (1987)

Silber, John: *Architecture of the Absurd. How "Genius" Disfigured a Practical Art.* The Quantutuck Lane Press, New York 2007

Simon, Madlen: *Design Pedagogy. Changing Approaches to Teaching Design.* In: Ockman, J. (ed.): *Architecture School. Three Centuries of Educating Architects in North America.* MIT Press 2012, 283

Tanizaki, Jun'ichiro: *In Praise of Shadows.* Leete´s Island Books 1977

Van Bruggen, Coosje: *Frank O. Gehry Guggenheim Museum Bilbao.* Guggenheim Museum Publications 2008

Zumthor, Peter: *Thinking Architecture.* Lars Müllers Publishers 1998, 9–21

7 Criticism

Criticism is not only interpretive and evaluative, it is also creative. (McAvin 1991, 156)

Criticism, to what end?

We would probably be very disturbed if, on our daily walk, we discovered that a house that had always been there was suddenly gone. Even if we had not paid it much attention, the house would still have been important for our experience of that street. Its disappearance would be alarming. We tend to take for granted that the world reveals itself in a certain way, because our senses react only when necessary, forcing us to re-evaluate a situation. Otherwise, we rely on stored sensory impressions and experiences.

Habitual situations do not develop our knowledge, but when something unexpected happens we have to stop and think about our choices. Experiences and thoughts are activated. However, John Dewey writes that reflections are not just a flow of ideas inspired by experience and knowledge; they are also thoughts, with their possible consequences. These reflective thoughts grow gradually and support each other—in order to avoid chaos. Every phase is a step from one thing to something else. For new experiences to be established, learning should be part of a cohesive process and it should have substantial subjective meaning.

Criticism, as used in architectural education, helps by questioning the habitual, focusing the ability to observe, and generating reflections. You can see the teacher's questions as conflicts between the different opinions that can emerge in jury reviews, but also as potential opportunities for a shift in perspective that can be used to increase knowledge. If a student gets stuck when designing, for example, a ceremonial building with a complicated program, a critic can help by showing the differences between ceremony and daily life, i.e. the essence of ceremony. The focus will thus be put on the fundamental aspects of ceremony: its movement and rhythm. The perspective of rhythm can have direct impact in a discussion on how a person approaches the building, step by step: the tactile expression of the ground surface, the entry and its dimensions, the lighting sources, and the places for pausing and changing direction. This can lead to reflections on choreographed movement, which can then inspire studies on the role of movement in traditional Japanese architecture. In doing so, a sterile analysis of function can be brought to life by concentrating on the essence of the activity.

Every project in an architecture program concludes with a final review ("the jury") and there is often an intermediate review for partial presentations during the course of the project (known as "pin-ups"). The guidance you receive in the design studio (a so-called "desk crit") is also a kind of criticism that helps you reflect on your proposal and assists you by showing other interpretations. Criticism is ever-present at architecture schools and in architectural offices. It develops the skill of coping with uncertainties which affect not only students, but even experienced professionals. The process of receiving criticism hones your judgment and helps you manage the complexity that is inherent in architecture and in the creative profession of the architect. This depends, of course, on how well the pedagogical potential of criticism is understood and utilized.

These days, architectural education and several other design educations are essentially based on the critique methodology that is part of the framework of the design studio. The periodic individual criticism that is applied in the studio is still known as the best way to teach architects to deal with uncertainty and complexity.

Some terms
The word *criticism*, in itself, is neutral, but a common perception is that it has a negative connotation. It comes from the Greek *kritikos*

(decisive) and *krino* (to judge). Together, it means the *art of judgment* – to make judgments or decisions based on particular criteria. Criticism is the positive or negative judgment of an object, a performance or behavior.

There are subtle differences in the way the word is used in relation to architecture. You can refer to *architectural criticism* and then you can talk about *criticism. Architectural criticism* and *critical studies* implies criticism focusing on the built environment and the process of creating architecture, and it is often found in architectural magazines and other media. Without the pretext "architectural", criticism is most frequently used in the sense of evaluating *proposals* for buildings or environments that are presented in education, in competitions, or for other proposals in different practical situations. Assessment reviews, also known as *critiques*, or juried reviews, are the basis of the pedagogical method in which students take turns presenting their proposals to a critic or a jury as well as to other students in the design studio.

It was hard to avoid thinking that the word *critique* (a "crit" in the jargon of architecture and design schools) and the associated, often threatening word *jury*, could exacerbate the stress levels of students. So, as part of the reform of the design studio culture in the 1990s in the USA, the previously used *jury* was replaced by the less threatening *review* (Anthony 2012, 400). The beginning of the British book *The Crit* starts by explaining:

> *This guide is called* The Crit *because that term is familiar to most people but we use the term 'review' throughout to promote the more positive aspects of the process.* (Parnell et al. 2007, 4)

In the same fashion, a recent intermediate review in the School of Architecture at the Royal Institute of Technology in Stockholm was given the name of the Swedish word for "balancing".

Presenting the collected research in a particular field, for instance, an overview of construction materials or the use of color in architecture, involves a systematic, possibly critical, delivery of knowledge that is mostly controllable. The same cannot be said of the criticism of student projects in the design studio or at reviews, because the level of complexity is so much higher, no matter what size the project is. Subjective interpretations of the problem and value judgments can hardly be avoided.

Another variation, the so-called *speed crit*, is a summary review with critics giving ad hoc reactions as they move quickly (three to five minutes per proposal) from one presentation to the next. The presenters stand next to their proposals so that they can answer possible questions. Neither the students nor the critics have time to reflect on balanced formulations of their viewpoints. A speed crit is mostly appropriate for an intermediate review; to mobilize efforts leading up to a final deadline. It can give an overview of the working situation in the studio, but the pedagogical importance is limited. Experiences of these types of critiques are described by Laura Willenbrock from Miami University in negative terms. The speed crit reinforced her impression that students need not just comments from their teachers, but encouragement from them to participate in a dialogue about their proposals.

Criticism, types and purposes

A primary purpose of criticism is to develop the subject of architecture in architectural education by reinforcing the *analysis by synthesis* methodology, because that is what leads to conscious, appropriate choices and therefore, good architectonic solutions.

At the comprehensive level, criticism can be *product* or *process oriented*. Criticism that is *product oriented* is focused on the presented proposal, its architectonic qualities, and the possibilities for getting it built. The opinions given relate to whether the solution is optimal in terms of the different aspects that are part of the complexity of the problem: i.e. durability, utility or aesthetics. *Process-oriented* criticism concentrates on the student's working methods, his or her evaluation of the problem, and the thought and reflection behind chosen solutions. *How you go about* finding a good answer; in other words, *learning to design* is the primary objective.

The question *why* is of great importance in this arena. Both product-oriented and process-oriented criticism have great *pedagogical potential*. The prerequisite is that it is delivered in a constructive way that shows how you can conquer uncertainties, rather than in a destructive manner that leaves students in confusion. *Constructive criticism* includes critical viewpoints as well as suggestions for revisions. This can be in the form of plain comments, not intended as "criticism" of the proposal, but as an attempt to develop it and lay the groundwork for deeper understanding. It is not meant to be a judgment.

Criticism can be based on different foundations. The architectural theorist Wayne Attoe categorizes and analyzes various types of architectural criticism, and the way it appears in mass media and in professional discourse, in his book *Architecture and Critical Imagination* (1978). The focus of his interest is architectural criticism of buildings and environments. He hardly touches on the subject of criticism in architectural education, but despite that, his main categories are often used indiscriminately by critics and even students in their verbal presentations in critiques. Attoe talks about *normative, interpretive* and *descriptive criticism.*

Normative criticism is based on a fixed standard, a fixed method, or a system of rules or doctrines that are part of the contemporary paradigm. Examples of this are the ancient Greek ideals of proportion, the doctrine of Modernism *form follows function,* or other doctrines like Robert Venturi's emphasis on a building program's *true* complexity. Traditional concepts that particular building types are appropriate for certain activities because of their specific appearance, like housing or school architecture, is also a normative expression. Presently there are not such clear normative doctrines for the concept of beauty, so trends have a decisive impact.

Interpretive criticism, which can be *defensive, associative* or *impressionistic*, is highly personal, and is an attempt to get other people to accept a vision that the critic or presenter has already decided on. External standards are less important in this type of criticism. The critic's credibility is more important than facts. Michael

Benedikt's campaign for an "architecture of reality"[1] or the case in Sweden, where the present debate on the restructuring of the Slussen area shows clear aspects of *defensive criticism*. *Associative criticism* expresses feelings by using suggestive images and photos as in, for example, when you show a city in sun or in fog, depending on the message you want to communicate. *Impressionistic criticism* can be merely the spontaneous viewpoints of the critics. Interpretive criticism can scarcely be considered objective, but it can help increase awareness of the object of criticism and therefore be of pedagogical value.

Descriptive criticism, which may be *figurative, biographical* or *contextual,* has the character of a report, with plain descriptions and no judgments. *Figurative descriptions* start with static aspects like form, material, finish, or from dynamic aspects: how a building is used, how it changes over time, and how it influences its surroundings. *Biographical criticism,* for example similar to the aforementioned description by Peter Blake of F.L. Wright's, Le Corbusier's and Mies van der Rohe's lives and architecture, connects the stories of buildings and environments to events in the designer's life. *Contextual criticism* attempts to widen the understanding of objects by relating them to social conditions, the economic and political context and any possible pressure that has been put on the designers during their work.

These categories are rarely seen clearly and independently in architectural criticism. The same is true in education, when students present their proposals, or when they encounter criticism from their tutors in the studio, in critiques in different levels, or at a juried review of thesis projects. Students generally use *interpretive criticism* when they talk about their understanding of a problem, and *descriptive criticism* when they make an actual presentation. It is worth reflecting on which type of criticism is chosen. If you want to emphasize the poetic dimensions of a proposal, an interpretive associative criticism may be appropriate, while the object's rational value may be illustrated with figurative criticism.

The main categories—*normative, interpretive and descriptive criticism*—are primarily formulated on a criticism of built environments. It is more difficult to criticize an architectural proposal than a built environment, because you have to evaluate *an idea* of something that as yet only exists as a representation. Built environments can be experienced with all your senses, and you can observe how they are used, which is impossible with only a proposal to look at. On the other hand, studying illustration drawings and models lets you immediately and simultaneously see the whole project, with all of the plans, elevations, and the relationship between inside and outside, including the construction of the walls and details, etc. This is difficult to grasp when you have the finished building or environment in front of you. Perceptions of *imaginary presence* and engaging with sensual values are of utmost importance in both the designer's presentation and in the commentary by the critics.

Historical roots

Kathryn H. Anthony (1991) has tracked public presentations of student work back to the 18th century in Cambridge, where a type of examination was followed by a disputation between younger and older students. This eventually developed into a process of delivering critical reviews with a ranking of the students. But even the earlier, previously mentioned, "visitors" chosen by the academy in 16th century Florence were a kind of criticism of student work that has been adopted, in modified form, by most design educations.

Today's architectural teaching is similar to the method that was established at the École Royale des Beaux Arts in the 19th century, when the teaching was accomplished in ateliers, corresponding to today's design studios, where there was both cooperation and competition between students. Older students were assigned to criticize the work of the younger students, and in return they received help with simpler tasks in their own projects.

There were many hard competitions. A design jury reviewed and graded the student work behind closed doors. Contrary to current practice, the projects were judged entirely on their graphic presentations. Verbal presentations were non-existent. A special rule of the system was that the student work was "defended" by the studio tutors, who were essentially defending their own status as educators. Students had to compete so that they could secure themselves important jobs in the future. The most prestigious and important competition was the Prix de Rome[2] which was administered in three steps involving a meticulous selection process. For the first step, 30 students were locked in a room for 12 hours to work on a relatively simple task, for instance, the design of a facade. A week later, they were given another assignment to solve within 24 hours. The weakest student proposals were eliminated after both step one and two. For the final, third step, eight students were chosen to develop proposals for a very difficult, complex building (Broadbent 1995). The tradition of the Prix de Rome endured and the 1899 winner was Tony Garnier, who is seen as a pioneer of city planning, not least for his ideas for the perfectly planned city, *Une ville industrielle.* The prize was finally terminated in 1968.

In the USA, the methodology of the design studio, with its teaching and critiques, came into fashion at the turn of the 20th century. From the 1930s onward, the critiques evolved from closed evaluations into open reviews in the presence of students, invited critics and other guests.[3] The Bauhaus teaching method was imported by Walter Gropius to the United States when he became Dean of the School of Architecture at Columbia University. Studio project learning, with cooperation and an open climate between students, replaced the Beaux Arts-style competitions. The student projects were often based on the needs of society.

In Sweden, the system of a project-based educational style, with teachers in different subjects cooperating with each other, was first used in the 1970s. A more developed, typical studio teaching method was then introduced at The KTH School of Architecture in Stockholm in the 1990s, and in approximately the year 2000 at the Chalmers School of Architecture in Gothenburg. Critiques of different kinds had already been in use a few decades earlier, but public defense of thesis projects was only introduced as late as the start of the 1990s. Presently desk crits and juried reviews or critiques are the main established structure for architectural education.

The previously mentioned strict distinction between evaluation and learning—part of the Beaux Arts tradition (summative and formative functions)—has gradually disappeared, but there can be problems when the edifying, pedagogical intent of the critique is mixed with the evaluation and grading of student work.

Tutoring and desk critique

You can see today's architectural education as an academic version of an apprentice system. In both cases, the important foundation for learning was, and is, *the doing*. In the apprentice system, a master craftsman showed how to do something, be it crafting a table or building a masonry wall. Only certain facets of the work could be explained verbally, since tacit knowledge was part of the skill. In contemporary design studios, it is the student who *does* things and the teacher who *reacts to* the student's proposal. But the situation is clearly more difficult now than during the time of the traditional apprentice, because the student is required to make independent attempts right from the start.

A relevant analogy is the practice of throwing non-swimmers into deep water to teach them to swim. In the current situation, criticism is an effective tool for illustrating the criteria that are important when choosing which idea to develop—out of several ideas that seem promising. You have to reflect on, and critically test, these ideas against a growing collection of criteria. The task of the "apprentice" or student is then to learn to be his or her own critic; to acquire a dynamically thinking professional judgment and confidence. The ability to criticize your own work is not only an important general aspect of education, but it is also of particular importance in the architectural profession, as was shown in a study done by The American Institute of Architects:

One of the most important "trade secrets" of firms that have achieved design excellence is the ability to critique their own work. Constructive board criticisms help them to continually refine and improve their design at many stages of the design process. (Anthony 1991, 163)

Design work means that when students are sitting at their desks, they have to initiate a dialog with themselves, their sketches, and with the situation surrounding the assignment. The teacher is another partner who participates in this conversation by approving or questioning the proposal at hand, and then providing constructive criticism. A review of several studies shows that desk crits in the studio are the type of criticism that students appreciate the most, and they are considered more productive than the criticism in juried reviews (critiques), which can seem very difficult for beginner-level students. Of this experience, Elizabeth Graham writes:

I remember how intimidated I was during my first design jury. I remember a classroom full of eyes on my project and myself. I was unprepared and I didn't know how to prepare because I didn't know what to expect. I hadn't slept the night before because I was up all night working frantically on my project. Honestly, I don't remember the grade I received on that project, or the feedback that was given to me during my jury. I do remember being relieved it was over, because I could go home and sleep and forget about the whole experience. (Graham 2003, 2)

Gradually the student learns that criticism can assist by showing that the assignment (like most design tasks) can contain *several possible interpretations of the problem* and therefore many possible solutions. This involves an element of risk, because the student's knowledge is usually insufficient. However, part of the essence of creativity is the need to take risks to create something new. So in this phase, the student is therefore encouraged to think fearlessly and test their solutions (qualified guesses) in order to better understand (and possibly re-formulate) the assignment and discover the constraints that may exist (range of possibilities). The whole process at this stage involves a somewhat tentative application of the *analysis by synthesis* method. A sensitive teacher develops an individual relationship to each student and responds to their proposals with careful suggestions on how to develop their ideas. The student gets help in discerning the important aspects, while their individual efforts are not ignored.

A simulated architect–client situation may also be seen as a form of criticism that results in increased involvement and a perception of what it would be like to use the proposed building. For example, this was the case when the first-year students were the architects, designing single-family homes, while the teachers from the other groups were the clients, providing their individual briefs based on their family situations and their own interests. The opportunity to discuss, for instance, special needs and wishes with the "client", like multigenerational arrangements, room for a grand piano, or the need for 100 meters of shelf space for a book collection made the assignment almost real and thus easier to grasp.

Assessment reviews

In tutoring and criticism in the studio, the students are limited by the boundaries created by their own proposals and their own interpretations of the assigned problem. That which is not brought up during tutoring and desk crits is not covered and may not be part of the student's awareness. In assessment reviews, however, many different aspects become accessible. The specifics of individual proposals show how you can handle complexity from different starting points.

The norm at the School of Architecture in Stockholm is that student participation is mandatory at assessment reviews. The entire student group in the upper years is a single design studio, but in the lower years, students are usually mixed from two different groups so that they can get a glimpse of how the teachers work in the other groups, as well as in their own. A student is in charge of timing so that each student gets the same amount of time for their critique. Two or three critics—teachers from other courses or other studios, or practicing architects—review and comment on the proposals in front of the student group. The group's own teacher is usually present, but this is not a requirement.

The tone and character of an assessment review can vary, depending on the academic level of the studio and the pedagogical principles used at a specific school. In the lower years, during the relatively short periods of assessment reviews, emphasis is placed on the aspects that help the students develop their three-dimensional thinking and their ability to alternate between a sensual and abstract relationship to their own proposals. The criticism given should also clarify and strengthen certain basic principles like open/closed, mass/void, structure, order/chaos, subjective/objective, etc., which may also be used in dichotomy games. Teaching the particular thought process of *analysis through synthesis*, with all its inherent openness and free association, can be more important than receiving training in manual or digital presentation techniques. At the same time, the ability to draw, by hand or on the computer, helps the student to express thoughts and make them available for critical review. It is appropriate to alternate between the abstract and the concrete and learn to use design work as a platform for generating ideas about life; in other words, to get the sense of being *present* in the project you are working on.

Criticism in the lower years should be more process oriented rather than product oriented, to introduce and instill the working method of analysis through synthesis.

The complexity of the projects increases in the upper years. Criticism can become more product oriented, based on sensitivity, aesthetics, functionality and technical systems, among other aspects. The discussion can then start to cover different values, and even social aspects in relation to various technical requirements. The clarity of a proposal and the choice of an appropriate presentation technique in relation to the project's character, the design stage it is at, and the ability of the audience to read the drawings, all become apparent. To engrain the instinctive use of *analysis through synthesis,* the students should use working sketches and models to show their deliberations during the project and alternative ways to look at the problem. Based on this material, a proposal can be further developed, giving the student and his or her classmates a chance to learn. This also leads to an understanding of which skills the student needs to augment. A critical assessment, done this way, makes the learning process dynamic.

Depending on the type of problem and the proposal, the critic's main questions can be: *where, what, if, why, how,* etc., all to illustrate the proposal's relationship to the constantly relevant Vitruvian concepts of durability, utility and beauty. The most helpful question is *why.* It can aid the student to build their foundation of values. *Why have you chosen to propose a massive building? Why are the building forms shaped like they are? Why is this chosen synthesis better than the other possible choices?* If the answer is: *because I like it that way,* this should generate a new *why.* This is similar to when Peter Zumthor asks himself what the architectural qualities are that cause a building to *move* him and how he can apply those qualities to his own proposals.[4]

A critical assessment can often yield uncertainties or ambiguity, because time was too limited, or if the critics could not formulate their comments well enough. For that reason, the studio tutor should arrange a session with the student group to review the critics' viewpoints and clarify and reiterate the constructive aspects of the criticism. In the lower years, it is very important to reinforce basic concepts as soon as they are introduced. A well-liked teaching method is to have a special lecture after the critical assessment session, with selected proposals shown on a large screen. The student proposals are not chosen in order to grade or select the best ones; they are used to illustrate different interpretations of the concepts that were introduced. For example, you can show the various ways in which students have "shaped" the architectonic space, and use this to demonstrate that an architect *always* has to think in three dimensions, which is not obvious to all students.

Critical assessments provide an overview of the level of the student group and in this way they give feedback on the effectiveness of the learning to date, which is of interest to the teachers as well as the students. A purely practical aspect is that work scheduling becomes clear. Considering all of the uncertainties of design, the process could drag on, but the realization that a deadline for submittal/ presentation of the proposal is approaching causes accelerated decision-making. Knowing when to stop designing is a skill that must be learned. For instance, in the 1980s, a single design project could go on for the entire school year, but the extended period did not result in enrichment; on the contrary, the students had a tendency to delay their decisions, causing exhaustion and reduced motivation. Most of the presented proposals were of a lower quality than the ones done after a two-and-a half-month time limit was established.

There are several pedagogical advantages in having critical assessments, both for students and teachers. A successful critique that emphasizes the design process:
- shows clearly that several solutions are possible
- opens a discussion about problem interpretation,
  concepts and criteria behind design choices
- reveals various sides to the problem for the entire
  student group
- leads to new viewpoints
- illustrates specific technical or social issues as necessary
- encourages discussions of conceptual questions,
  the role of the architect, etc.

There are opportunities in both the process- and product-oriented criticism to:

- enrich the architectural debate and introduce discussions using the terminology of architectural theory
- present references, thereby widening the architectural vocabulary
- acquire new knowledge, reflect on disparate values and gradually cover larger areas of skill and competency
- see if the chosen presentation technique succeeds in communicating the message and get advice on alternative presentation methods.

Critical assessment also has important psychological implications because it:
- gives the student feedback, opinions and encouragement
- relieves the uncertainty of what the "correct" solution is by clarifying important criteria
- contributes to a positive studio atmosphere by reinforcing the learning process.

A critical assessment is often experienced as a severe kind of test, where not only is the student's knowledge and talent evaluated, but his or her self-identity can be strained to the limit. The critique situation is frequently very tense, especially if the student is being graded simultaneously. The students agonize about the comments and are often uncertain if their solution is appropriate. A long period of work concludes with a final exertion. The critic's task is not simple, either. They must have a distinct ability to quickly assess several proposals and be able to summarize their strengths and weaknesses on a large and small scale, in a relevant and constructive way. The tense atmosphere means that the learning potential inherent within the process of critique is not always fully utilized.

Final examination by jury

Architecture studies usually finish formally after five years with a final examination consisting of the presentation and open defense of a proposal for a complex building or urban design. The complexity is not necessarily defined by a complicated brief, size or scale; there may be opportunities for developing minor or artistic aspects of the problem. One of the most competent thesis projects I have encountered through the years was a sauna, only 20 square meters (200 square feet) that a student designed for their aunt. The proposal contained the whole spectrum of architectonic thinking in terms of floor, walls, ceiling, roof, the feeling of approach and arrival, material finishes and their tactile qualities, and also technical aspects like slender structures, water supplies from a nearby lake, etc.

Examination days, for example, in Sweden and in Denmark, are scheduled once or twice per academic year. Prior to that the individual students submit their proposed projects to their studio teachers, outlining the subjects/problems they want to work with. Depending on which projects the student has undertaken during their earlier studies, the proposal will be approved, or an alternative direction recommended. The student formulates a program and a short description, and after that they have a total of 100 days for the design and completion of their final proposal. During this period, a couple of seminars are held. At both of these seminars, project work may be interrupted if it is clear that the student will not be able to develop their proposal sufficiently for approval in the remaining time period. After the final seminar, there should only be refinement and final presentation work taking place.

The examination jury generally consists of three external jury members who, together, have experience from well-known design practices, but also of teaching at schools of architecture in other countries. A brief description of every project is sent in advance to the jury members, so that they can familiarize themselves with the type of proposal that will be presented. This also gives the students a chance to show their ability to summarize, which is an essential, and often decisive, skill in the architect's professional practice. The final proposals are presented as 2D visuals, models, and/or digital media in seminar rooms or studios prior to the examination sessions.

The actual procedure is similar to the one used during critical assessments, but the stress level is much higher because the presentations are public and open to all those who are interested. The audience, which can vary from 10 to 50 depending on the amount of interest sparked by the project, is made up of teachers, students from lower years, and the student's family and friends. The student being tested presents his or her proposal and then the jury comments on it; occasionally someone in the audience joins the discussion.

The student should focus on making a vivid presentation. It is much better to explain what you will see and how you react when you *step into* the building or environment than to talk about functional details that are already shown in the drawings. For example, you can consciously use *figurative* descriptions for static or dynamic aspects as well as mood-inducing *interpretive associative* descriptions to generate emotions in the audience. Video and audio-visual input can complement the presentation, but giving a *purely* digital presentation is not appropriate because then neither the jury members nor the audience can see the entire project both in its entirety, and with its individual details *simultaneously*. It is probable that such a digital presentation, and the resultant critique, will be fragmented. On the other hand, digital presentations can be valuable as complements, especially for diagrams and general issues.

The jury will often start by asking questions about things that are unclear, and then go on to give summaries of their viewpoints. The questions can be very diverse, for example: *What is your strategy for the entire area? Why do you choose this building material? How do you ensure fire safety in multi-storey buildings?* From a pedagogical viewpoint, the final examination is the school's last chance to teach and instill confidence in the students before they enter professional practice. However, you can also see it as a kind of journeyman's test. In both cases, the balance—between focusing on the product and focusing on the process—is crucial.

Research on assessment reviews

In the preceding section, assessment reviews were described with an examination of their learning potential and how they can succeed in making the *analysis through synthesis* method complete and manageable. However, the available research poses the question as to whether the considerable pedagogical potential of criticism in architectural education is not always utilized, and that which should be criticism's main purpose—to show students how to manage and subdue uncertainty—can sometimes fail. One of the reasons is the way in which the assessment review is seen as an opportunity to judge, evaluate and grade the students, which is hard to combine with its pedagogical goals. Marking and grading tend to encourage so-called external motivation in the hunt for higher grades, instead of internal motivation, which is of great importance in individual development. This can lead to competition and discourage cooperation between students in the studio. Grading can also cause anxiety, reducing the critique's pedagogical value, which will be discussed below.

An architecture school's norms, cultural climate and rituals are very important indicators of the education there and the results that follow. There are a few texts available about the critique process that provide basic advice on how a student can avoid getting nervous during an assessment review; for example, by organizing their work and by not working for several nights in a row before the deadline. You can also find good advice about presentations: *"Avoid sexist/racist stereotypes. For example, assuming every client is a white man"* (Parnell et al. 2007, 58). But all of these factors, even if they are fundamentally important, should be fairly easy to improve at the schools where they have not already been noticed in routine evaluations. The role of the critic is seldom discussed in the referenced literature, aside from quotes from disgruntled students. The behavior of the critic, which often determines whether an assessment review will be a valuable lesson or an embarrassing experience, is rarely scrutinized.

Actually, very few studies have been done on assessment reviews, despite the fact that international interest in the pedagogy of architectural education has increased after Donald Schön illustrated the relationship between teachers and students in a design studio. Kathryn H. Anthony's comprehensive empirical study, where she asked about the pedagogical value of intermediate and final critiques and how students cope with public criticism, is one of the exceptions. Also, a smaller study into the education of landscape architects done by E.M. Graham at Louisiana State University analyzes the expectations of teachers and students prior to critical assessments, as well as the results of those critical assessments. The book, *The Crit: An Architecture Student's Handbook* by Rosie Parnell and Rachel Sara et al. is primarily aimed at giving good advice to students and suggesting certain changes in critique routines. Furthermore, a study done by Jeremy Lowe in the late 1960s still has relevance, even though it was specifically oriented toward a type of criticism that is less common now, namely a jury evaluation of submitted material behind closed doors, without students present.[5]

Several of these texts contain quotes with negative opinions and strongly critical voices from teachers and students, but there are also some positive judgments. Some studies suggest different routines for critical assessments; mostly organizational changes. An anthology compiled by Thomas Dutton focuses on the power structure in a design studio and includes proposals for modifying the process of assessment reviews. In one of the essays in the anthology, Laura L. Willenbrock describes assessment reviews from the student's perspective. This student experience of assessment reviews is depicted in other writings by architects.

The interest in this process has grown among educators recently. A doctoral thesis on the subject was submitted in 2010 by the pedagogue Gustav Lymer at the University of Gothenburg. Lymer is aware of the complexity of the architectural profession, he appreciates the architect's working method, and he emphasizes the pedagogical value of assessment reviews:

Critique is a setting in which practical grammars of seeing,
saying, and doing are defined, coordinated, and taught.
(Lymer 2010, 171)

The most comprehensive study in the field, by Kathryn H. Anthony (1991), was undertaken in two phases. Several hundred architectural students participated in phase 1,[6] which included observations, questionnaires and interviews. A general questionnaire was also given to architecture students (n=85) at a medium-sized American university. Teachers and alumni also took part. Phase 2 involved a follow-up at other universities and a comparison between the sub-culture of architecture students and students in other disciplines.

Anthony's study covered the following questions:
1 What educational value do critiques have, and for whom (current and earlier students' and teachers' evaluations)? Comparisons between criticism in education and presentations in professional practice; are critiques good training for presentations? Can critiques be improved, and if so, how?
2 Are intermediate and final critiques equally effective educationally?
3 How do students cope with critiques?
4 What do the students' behavioral patterns look like?

A large majority of students, teachers and practicing architects thought that assessment reviews needed improvement. Students thought that intermediate and final critiques had different goals. They believed that overall they did not learn much from critiques, but if at all, more from intermediate critiques (which gave more ideas) than from final critiques. Desk crits were considered the most valuable, while final crits were thought to be the least valuable. The students believed that they learned more about how to play the game in crits, rather than about design. They also expressed that the critics were often too self-centered, and their contradictory statements could cause frustration. They believed that the critique gave no adequate feedback when the critics just praised "a good proposal" without explaining which qualities were exemplary.

The students who had positive feelings in connection with critiques were in a minority. On a scale from 1 to 5, desk crits were rated 4, final critiques of their own proposal 3.3 and final critiques of other students' proposals 3.43.

A smaller study (n=51) done by Michael Seymour (2008) confirms Anthony's results about how desk crits and tutoring in the studio are considered most valuable by students because of their "effectiveness" and "helpfulness", and also because they give motivation, encouragement and understanding. The least appreciated types of criticism were the less common self-evaluations. However, Seymour states that his study confirms that every type of criticism has certain advantages. Even if students prefer individual discussions with their own teacher because they are least stressful psychologically, traditional assessment reviews with a jury give fulfillment by involving a different kind of presentation than in other types of critiques.

The inspiration for E.M. Graham's study (2003) came from her own experience of critiques. She explains her own feeling of having her ego destroyed as a first-year student, when she expected approval for a proposal she was proud of, but was instead sharply criticized and told to take an entirely different direction. Later, as a teacher, she wanted to find out:

1 What are teachers trying to achieve through the process of criticism in the studio and in the assessment review?
2 How do students experience these situations?

Her results showed that approximately half of students said that teachers rarely explained the goals of the critique. Almost as many felt that assessment reviews should be for the good of the presenting student and other participants, but only one-fifth felt that this was actually true. The students had expectations based on educational critiques; they thought that the jury would give them different viewpoints, but these expectations were often not met. In reality, students frequently had only their own teacher as a critic.

The previously mentioned authors Dutton, and Parnell et al. state that critics use their power to force students to obey the conformity of the architectural profession—with the purpose of making students follow authoritarian perceptions of professional identity, without respect for the students' own identities. The entire scenario surrounding assessment reviews, with critics sitting in the front row, expounding in their own jargon, is thought merely to be a way to dominate students.

> *The relationship between presenter and listener is made problematic by the unequal relations of power between the two. This is supported by the unequal spatial arrangements, the number of listeners in relation to presenters, the structure, which favours tutor voices, and also, of positions of authority that tutors and visiting critics have in relation to the students (not least because they tend to hold the power of assessment).*
> (Parnell et al. 2007, 136)

In the opinion of the above authors, critical assessments are thus a manifestation of the power of the critic over the student. However, this viewpoint relies on generalizations that must be seen as dubious, considering how dependent the whole activity is on individuals. If it really were a power demonstration, then it must be due to failures of school policy, improper choices of critics, and/or of the critics' misunderstanding of their pedagogical tasks.

Anthony's study also incorporated the reflections of some well-known American architects (n=29), including thoughts on assessment reviews that they participated in as students. Looking back, a large majority (approx. 80%) of these architects considered assessment reviews to be a good or very good teaching method. However, they also expressed critical viewpoints. Some believed that presentations during an assessment review were entirely different than presentations for a client. Professional designers seem to get greater respect from clients than students get from a jury.

"Critiques are harder to deal with than a client presentation … your ego and your self-identity is more exposed."…"Critiques at school are a joke compared to, for example, budget meetings." There were several alumni who thought it was important to learn to present as if it was a rehearsal for an upcoming client presentation. But several also mentioned the pedagogical value of assessment reviews. Joseph Esherick[7] pointed out, for instance, that critics often focus on the assignment's final product, without any interest in how the student got there, and without contributing constructively to the student's further studies.

The oft-mentioned study by Anthony was done over 20 years ago; Graham's almost 10. You can consider their findings as an indicator of how assessment reviews *could* take place, but they cannot be considered entirely true now, since the climate at architecture schools, which affects the whole educational situation, is dynamic—meaning that new teachers develop new traditions and new students arrive with new demands. On the whole, it is difficult to generalize about assessment reviews, because every proposal that is presented is unique, as is every assessment review. Each critic is an individual; different than other critics. But even if critics can learn to be more sensitive, there can still be those who are inappropriate; who fail to recognize the pedagogical goals of assessment reviews. It is the responsibility of every architecture school to rectify this, because this difficult task, of teaching the art of coping with uncertainty in the face of complexity, is so dependent on how the critics interpret the goals of assessment reviews and their own role in them. The critic's professional and pedagogical skills can, in the end, be a decisive factor in the students' ability to develop their own critical attitude, which is so essential to the *analysis through synthesis* method.

Notes

References

1 Benedikt's concepts of real architecture are: presence, significance, materiality and emptiness (1987).
2 The "Prix de Rome" was a scholarship for art students in the fields of sculpture, painting and architecture created in France in 1663 by Ludvig XIV. The prize was terminated in 1968.
3 The majority of architecture schools changed over to this system, mainly in the 1940s and 1950s: Anthony (1991).
4 Zumthor (2006, 11): "Quality architecture to me is when a building manages to move me. What on earth is it that moves me? How can I get it to my work?"
5 Hall Jones (1996) refers to Lowe, J.: *The Assessment of Students' Architectural Design Drawings* (1969).
6 Behavioral observations of 130 students, interviews with 43 students immediately after critiques and with 43 during coursework, questionnaires from 189 students, and 27 daily journals.
7 Joseph Esherick was one of the founders of Berkeley's College of Environmental Design (CED).

Anthony, Kathryn H.: *Design Juries on Trial, the Renaissance of the Design Studio*, Van Nostrand Reinhold, New York 1991, 9, 163–199, 241
Anthony, Kathryn, H.: *Studio Culture and Student Life. A World of Its Own.* In: Ockman, Joan (ed.): *Architecture School. Three Centuries of Educating Architects in North America.* MIT Press 2012, 400
Attoe, Wayne: *Architecture and Critical Imagination.* John Wiley & Sons Ltd. 1978, 74–106
Benedikt, Michael: *For an Architecture of Reality.* Lumen Books 1987
Blake, Peter: *The Master Builders.* London, Victor Gollancz Ltd. 1960
Broadbent, Geoffrey: *Architectural Education.* In: Pearce, Martin; Toy, Maggie (eds): *Educating Architects.* Academy Editions, London 1995, 15
Dewey, John: *How We Think.* Dover Publications Inc. 1997 (1910), 2
Dutton, Thomas: *Architectural Education and Society*: An Interview with J. Max Bond Jr. In: Dutton, Thomas A. (ed.): *Voices in Architectural Education. Cultural Politics and Pedagogy.* Bergin & Garvey,

New York 1991a

Dutton, Thomas A. (ed.): *Voices in Architectural Education. Cultural Politics and Pedagogy*. Bergin & Garvey, New York 1991b

Dutton, Thomas: *The Hidden Curriculum and the Design Studio: Toward a Critical Studio Pedagogy*. In: Dutton, Thomas A. (ed.): *Voices in Architectural Education. Cultural Politics and Pedagogy*. Bergin & Garvey, New York 1991c

Graham, Elizabeth Marie: *Studio Design Critique: Student and Faculty Expectations and Reality*. A Thesis. The School of Landscape Architecture. Christian Brothers University 2003, 2

Hall Jones, Sue: *Crits - An Examination*. Journal of Art & Design Education, Vol. 4, 1996, 133–141

Lymer, Gustav: *The work of critique in architectural education*. Doctoral thesis. Studies in Educational Sciences 298. Göteborgs Universitet 2010, 171

McAvin, Margaret: *Landscape Architecture and Critical Inquiry: Introduction*. Landscape Journal, Vol. 10, No. 2, 1991, 156

Parnell, Rosie and Sara, Rachel with Doidge, Charles & Parsons, Mark: *The Crit: An Architecture Student's Handbook*. Elsevier Science & Technology Books 2007

Pearce, Martin; Toy, Maggie (eds): *Educating Architects*. Academy Editions, London 1995

Seymour, Michael: *Beginning Design Students´ Perception of Design Evaluation Techniques*. National Conference on the Beginning Design Student. Proceedings 2008

Willenbrock, Laura L.: *An Undergraduate Voice in Architectural Education*. In: Dutton, Thomas A. (ed.): *Voices in Architectural Education. Cultural Politics and Pedagogy*. Bergin & Garvey, New York 1991, 103

Zumthor, Peter: *Atmospheres. Architectural Environments. Surrounding Objects.* Birkhäuser–Publishers for Architecture, Basel 2006

8 Assessment reviews: stage and actors

Creative personality

The eccentric behavior of creative individuals, sometimes seen as arrogance, is a source of modern myth. Ayn Rand's book *The Fountainhead* may have reinforced the (mis)conception that an architect is an odd character whose only goal is to realize his or her artistic visions. Can people like that really alternate between humility and self-confidence; between sensitivity and professionalism?

What characterizes creative people became a hot research topic, after the 1950s discovery that creativity is something very different than intelligence measured by standard IQ tests. What interested psychologists, social psychologists and organization researchers most was the subject of creativity and inventiveness. Several studies were directed at identifying creative people and investigating their personalities. In many cases, architects and architectural education came under special scrutiny. Of great interest was the fact that architects are able to deal with great technical complexity in their work, even though their choices and decisions cannot always be based on an objective analysis of facts; they must often depend on their intuition and their own ethical/aesthetic beliefs. Numerous researchers into creativity recognized the complex character of the architecture profession in the following decades. For example, D.W. MacKinnon, head of the Institute of Personality Assessment and Research (IPAR) in Berkeley, California, carried out research on highly creative professionals like military pilots, engineers, architects and businesspeople, among others. He found that an architect needed to possess and combine many qualifications and skills:

> *The successful and effective architect must, with the skill of a juggler, combine, reconcile, and exercise the diverse skills of*

businessman, lawyer, artist, engineer, and advertising man, as
well as those of author and journalist, educator, and psychologist.
(MacKinnon, cited by Schoon 1992, 9)

After extensive research, MacKinnon produced results which showed that creative architects are characterized by strong independence, powerful decision-making ("they can stand firm") and social effectiveness. They show a strong desire to exert control over others, they ignore external limitations, they are free from paralyzing conventional inhibitions, and they yearn for tasks that require autonomous thoughts and actions. They are not concerned about the impression they make on other people.

In addition, psychologist Ingrid Schoon, who wrote her thesis on the subject of creativity at Leiden University in 1992, chose the field of architecture for her empirical studies of creativity because "*in architectural design we find a most general and comprehensive example of creative activity*" (1992, 8). Her doctoral thesis contains analyses of many creativity theories and comprehensive empirical studies. Her conclusion is that creativity cannot be understood if you divide a creative process into distinct, separate steps. This coincides with the aforementioned results from design research. The creative process can only be comprehended as a function of the whole person's interaction with a given situation because it depends on how the person perceives, organizes and interprets his or her surroundings. It should be understood as a balanced dialog between the individual and the context, between subjective desires and wishes and requirements from reality. The creative process is nourished by experience, but it reaches for a new situation; it changes the past, present and future. Even the previously mentioned D.W. MacKinnon recommends studying the architectural profession to better understand creativity, since:

It is in architects, of all our samples, that we can expect to find
what is most generally characteristic of creative persons...
in architecture, creative products are both an expression of the

architect, and thus a very personal product, and at the same time an impersonal meeting of the demands of an external problem.
(Cited by Lawson 2008, 151)

Ingrid Schoon examined and formulated psychological profiles of a group of architecture students by using three method types, namely:

1 Standardized questionnaires and projective tests.[1]
2 Observations and surveillance of the same group's behavior in the design studio.
3 Dynamic analysis techniques for finding patterns indicated by individual case studies.

Based on these comprehensive studies carried out by herself and others, she determined that creative individuals are unwilling to accept stereotypical conventions and quickly seek out a new, unknown and often controversial response. They reject the easier consensus and give their own subjective opinion. They are open to their inner landscape, i.e. their subjective (sometimes irrational) thought processes. Psychology professor Gudmund Smith says that our conscious sensations are well organized and arranged for our everyday use. Opening up to inward communication, into less ordered and more emotionally driven layers, can open the door to chaos and cause worry and anxiety. Creative people are very tolerant of such anxiety and they are capable of summoning and utilizing their inner drive in a controlled way. They can organize complex information and seemingly incompatible expressions and ideas into new, integrated concepts which can be meaningful for themselves and for a wider audience. Their creative accomplishments are not just a result of being open to subjectivity; they depend instead on a balanced dialog between the objective world of conventions and the subjective arena of preferences and desires.

Numerous researchers have found that architects and architecture students generally have a high level of *cognitive* skill, but there has been no significant correlation found between traditional intelligence tests and architecture students' creative abilities. Architecture students tend to have more visual than verbal intelligence, a high degree of flexibility, and a preference for complexity. Their judgment is guided equally by aesthetic values and by rational truth-seeking and involvement. They can cope with the tension caused by conflicting interests and contradictory information. The more creative students show a greater autonomy, they are more often non-conforming, and they have a greater tendency to abandon conventional patterns of social values and behavior than those less creative students. To initiate a creative process and formulate a problem (where others see nothing), or defend a proposal in debates or during a critique, it is essential for creative individuals, states I. Schoon, that they must be independent and determined, they must believe in their own ideas and values (and take them seriously), and exhibit endurance and perseverance.

More than others, creative people often experience *their feelings and thoughts working in concert*. Otherwise, civil engineer Dag Romell (1974) has written in his book, *Kreativitet—en outnyttjad resurs* (Creativity—an Under-utilized Resource), that it is a typical preconception that emotions and reason are in conflict in this rational world and time. He refers to statistical studies focusing on people who were involved with technical inventions, and who were characterized by exhibiting constructive creativity, i.e. creativity bounded by constraints, in contrast to free creativity. The results show that constructive creativity is found in only a small percentage of the population. Architects are not mentioned specifically in relation to this, but their creative work is similar to that of the study group since it is also bound by numerous constraints.

Based on his research, MacKinnon described architects as polite, well-adapted and highly effective people. But there is also a view of creative architects that is not so flattering. In addition to Ayn Rand's book *The Fountainhead*, quotes from Peter Blake's *The Master Builders*, a critical biography of three famous architects, have reinforced these judgments. Blake portrays Frank Lloyd Wright as arrogant, strident and conceited, Mies van der Rohe as shy, quiet and extremely self-disciplined, and finally Le Corbusier as cold, suspicious, combative, sarcastic and humorless; arrogant to most, but charming to those who knew him and to people when he first met them. Adding to the generalizations based on Blake's text, psychologist Ian MacFarlane Smith depicts a creative architect as a thoroughly unsympathetic individual: asocial, lacking humor, cold, calculating, self-centered, rigid, reticent, etc. However, his study was actually not primarily directed at architects (who, together with engineers were part of one out of nine test groups), but generally concentrated on spatial ability. Ten renowned architects, including Gropius, Mackintosh and Le Corbusier, among others, were chosen as those:

who appear to have exhibited high spatial ability together with
well marked schizothymic or schizoid traits (as far as could
be judged from biographical accounts or from portraits).
(MacFarlane Smith 1964, 321 and 330)

However, judging personality traits of architects from Blake's descriptions and portraits should be considered questionable. Even with great effort it is difficult to form any generalizations from this material. But there are other authors, with no scientific ambitions or need to generalize, who nonetheless are sharply critical of the inflated ambition and behavior of Le Corbusier and other named architects.[2]

Presumably, architects can be both courteous and discourteous in their efforts to be independent. What they do need in larger portions than in other professions is the ability to fluctuate between being receptive and humble on one side and then very confident when formulating solutions. Being just humble or just confident can only create uncertainty and rigidity. Switching between these attitudes should be a trait of good pedagogs; teachers and critics in architectural education who have to approach students with humility in order to understand how they think and to gauge their ability.

It is also the teacher's responsibility to help the students to adopt for themselves this method of fluctuating from humble to confident.

Those people who take part in critique situations—students, teachers and critics—have one thing in common: they are either in architectural training or they have gone through it. In their daily work, they use their creativity—that special ability to see new possibilities within conventional, habitual patterns. Another trait that most of them have is a strong need for independence—which can create tensions.

> *The truly creative individual has an image of himself as a responsible person with a sense of destiny about himself as a human being. This includes a degree of resoluteness and almost inevitably a measure of egotism. But over and above these there is a belief in the foregone certainty of the worth and validity of one's creative efforts. This is not to say that our creative subjects have been spared periods of frustration and depression when blocked in their creative striving, but only that over-riding these moods has been an unquestioning commitment to their creative endeavour.* (D. W. MacKinnon from "Genius and Eminence")[3]

Students

Students—creative individuals with a great need for autonomy—can be plagued by various uncertainties (see Chapter 1). Generally they are not prepared for an education that is completely different than what they are accustomed to. They also do not know that uncertainty is part of the creative process (see Chapter 4). Different ideas among the students about what design is can also create a degree of confusion in architectural education, according to Mark Gelernter (1995), well known for his excellent teaching methods. Students with creative, intuitive personalities prefer to do the opposite of what is expected of them, and they can feel that the special intuition you need to become an architect is something you are born with.

They feel that architectural education has limited value for them; that it can supplement their natural talent, but never provide creative ability if the innate qualities are lacking. Others may think that there is nothing new under the sun and that the designer's role is just to discover it (which coincides with the concept of redesign as explained in Chapter 6). These students tend to think that the education need not be very difficult for intelligent people; that it should just provide methods for observing the world in a rational way. Then there are those students who choose to not ask questions, and they lose the chance to understand quickly what their education is about. Finally, there are the students who want to ingratiate themselves with the teacher, and they may avoid taking independent risks. This is an undesirable reaction, as a teacher from Louisiana State University confirms:

The worst student is one who tries to please you, when you are trying to reflect back to the student what you see in the student and the student has nothing or is hiding what they think and instead trying to please you. (Graham 2003, 36)

The different personality traits of the students and their conception of what design is can either help or hinder their ability to handle criticism. Initially, there can be a misconception, sometimes subconscious, that the critique will not only focus on the presented proposal, but that it also includes criticism of the presenter.

Unfortunately, a bad critic can reinforce this impression. I recall a beginner student's severe reaction after a barrage of criticism, when he asked: *But what should I do now? How can I continue?* The critic—a respected architect—suggested, after some thought, that the best thing to do was to take down the proposal, throw it away, and start all over again. Actually, this opinion was not surprising in the sense that the architect's method, *analysis through synthesis*, involves doing sketches, reviewing them, rejecting parts, keeping others to develop and so on. But it was also poor pedagogical practice because the critic did not realize that the student had not yet learned that redoing sketches is standard procedure. Furthermore, the answer did not illustrate any possible criteria to help in coping with the complexity of the problem, which would have been useful for the entire group. The situation was very distressing for the affected student and he felt that he was thoughtlessly dismissed as a person in front of the whole class, and that was particularly painful.

The discussion during an assessment review should concentrate on the presented proposal and its making, the architectonic issues the proposal raises, the verbal and graphic presentations, physical models, etc. The difficult aspect for the students is to be able to step away from their own proposals and be objective. They commit themselves wholeheartedly to their projects and have a tendency to identify themselves with their proposals during the weeks or months of intense work. It is not a myth that architecture students work at night and that normal daytime hours are not enough. This is criticized by student organizations, among others, but the problem is difficult to solve when you schedule the same deadlines for a whole class or group of students. In other words, the assignments may be identical, but individual students take different amounts of time to complete them. They each have a different way of working. It is often the student's own ambition (or uncertainty) that delays the necessary decision-making, and maybe the student is waiting for a better idea to materialize than what he or she already has.

The fear of embarrassing yourself in front of the critics and your fellow students is imminent. It is very easy to experience negative criticism as personal criticism. This attitude can be aggravated if the project is being graded, leading to timid, rather than daring, proposals. It is common that beginner students, who initially seem to be struggling, become very successful later on when they begin to understand the *analysis through synthesis* method, which gives them the courage to test different solutions. They become accustomed to formulating solutions on uncertain grounds. They become aware that even a wrong guess can lead them to a learning experience. Getting lost in the search is the privilege of the student.

As mentioned earlier, the rate of progress from experiential level to fully autonomous level varies with the individual. The 29 successful architects who were interviewed in Kathryn H. Anthony's study were also asked how they ranked their own results during their education. Of those who answered the question, over 40 percent felt that they had weak results (some of them did improve in the upper years), several saw themselves as average, while just over 25 percent thought they did very well. Three of the latter architects stated clearly that they were very good at synthesis and design; one of them thought that the other students and teachers considered him a star student. At the time of the interview, all of the participating architects were well established, with several interesting projects built. Many of them were acting as visiting critics at architecture schools. Some of the leading architects emphasized that it takes longer to mature as a designer than the time available during education; one of them felt that it was inappropriate to enter architecture school at the age of 17–18, since life experience is essential in design work.

Depending on their particular personality traits and their different conceptions of the design process, students can accept criticism from studio tutors or visiting critics in different ways. Some students are open to other viewpoints; they reflect on them, and learn by doing so. This does not mean that they blindly accept their critics' suggestions for possible revisions; however, they take part in the discussion or listen attentively, then come to their own conclusions and do what they think is best. All opinions can open up new lines of thought, help to change direction, or reinforce the feeling that you are on the right path, but the final choices result from the independent decisions of the student. In that way, the student adopts a mature attitude and expects the same from the critics. Nevertheless, some creative students can barricade themselves in opposition and simply regard the critics and their viewpoints as fundamentally worthless. Even if the critics' opinions are faulty, the student loses an opportunity to see their proposal from a different perspective.

The mystique that numerous authors apply to the design process can be reduced somewhat if we look at the method of *analysis through synthesis* as a *qualified guess*, with all of the hazards that guesses connote. The chance of finding the right answer to any kind of riddle is improved if you have a broad knowledge in different fields that can provide inspiration and guidance. Personal preferences and experiences can spark the desire to experiment and to engage in independent expression. Some guesses are more accurate than others, but discussing this during a critique helps you identify and understand the criteria that you have to consider. This gradually adds awareness and knowledge, en route to professional competency at the autonomous level described previously.

Students need encouragement to experiment, by designing according to their convictions and interests. Kees Dorst (2006), Professor in Design, says that very talented students do not usually get good results during their education. They work independently and often seem to be on a collision course with their school system and with society in general. However, their independence is an element of their creativity.

Teachers

It is a privilege to be a teacher at a school of architecture. Not because it offers status, not because it is well paid (which it isn't), but because you have an opportunity to be part of a stimulating milieu among interesting people and talented students. Quite often I have heard teachers from other faculties complaining about their students' lack of motivation and participation. That is not the case when teaching architecture. Most students perceive it as a challenge to tirelessly seek out and produce solutions for their assignments. Finding the keys to each student's set of skills and their way of thinking requires the full mobilization of the teacher's creativity. A comprehensive curriculum provides enough leeway so that the teacher's independence is not infringed. The greatest reward for a teacher is to see the students' growth in awareness and to witness the progress they make.

Most of the teachers at architecture schools start their teaching careers based on their work experience from architectural firms and/ or academic accreditation, plus their innate ability to teach. Teaching the architectural method, *analysis through synthesis,* and the flexible thinking it requires, is a difficult task. The teacher's opportunities for pedagogic development and for reflection are usually minimal, and it is not always easy for a new teacher to know what to do.

The teaching skills of experienced and competent designers do not always match their designing skills. However, it is precisely a teacher's ability to teach that students seem to value the most. About half of the students who participated in a questionnaire presented in Belkis Uluoglu's doctoral thesis (2000) at Istanbul Technical University thought that the teacher's pedagogical ability was the most important factor in studio education; approximately one-third thought it was the teacher's personality; while only 16 percent considered exceptional design skills to be important.

To find out what is special about the teaching done by outstanding educators, 20 American teachers, who had been awarded various prizes for their excellent teaching, were interviewed.[4] It emerged that they could adopt three different roles; namely coach, advisor or parent. In a coach-teacher role, they made strong suggestions about what the students should do in order to reach their goals, and they could be sharp critics if necessary. In an advisory-teacher role, they were mostly focused on helping students discover and express their own latent design abilities. In a parent-teacher role, they had a general caring attitude and were interested in the students' basic development and welfare. The teachers who were interviewed felt that their work vitalized them and contributed to their identity. They were intensely engaged in their subjects and design methods, and their enthusiasm spread to their students. The method they used was more about asking and questioning than explaining or lecturing. Their questions provoked the students' interest in research.

A teacher should be aware of which knowledge and abilities the student needs to develop in order to progress from the experiential level to the autonomous level of the professional designer. Some architecture schools have a distinct culture which indicates the direction students must take. Most teachers educate others in the same way they were educated, but there are those who question their own experience and introduce new approaches. Teachers who stick to *one* educational doctrine and who are not receptive can encounter problems as a teacher. A high degree of flexibility is essential for dealing with any problem that may present itself. Some students can become more aware and fully engaged in their projects by using literary or poetic expressions, others by looking at them in a technical way. The question that a teacher must answer is: *Does the student understand criticism? Can you develop a conversation?* It can take some time for the student to realize that you can hardly create a comprehensive foundation to use in solving an assignment. In the design studio, *learning on a need to know basis* is an answer to the uncertainties that arise. Not only do the students expand their knowledge in this process; the teachers do also.

According to researchers in the field of creativity, architecture students are high on the scale of *cognitive ability*; they possess more visual than verbal intelligence, a high level of flexibility and a preference for complexity. At the individual level, though, different combinations of the intelligence types labeled by Howard Gardner may be present (see also Chapter 4). For the students to initiate a creative process and formulate a problem—when others don't notice anything—a teacher must have the skill to respect the students' different talents and individual ways of thinking. Donald Schön (1990) wrote that the student has to learn to listen operatively, imitate with their own thinking, and reflect on the teacher's and their own work process (knowing-in-action).

The lack of definitive answers is not only hard for the students, as described in the first chapter, but also for the teachers. One of the teachers at Louisiana State University says:

> *Initially they [the students] get frustrated because they want me to give them the answers. It's disconcerting for them to learn*

that there aren't any. They have to come up with the answer, they have to find it in themselves, it is a process. It's difficult because everywhere in school prior to this you can find the answer in a book (interview). (Graham 2003, 36)

Presumably, there are few teachers now who believe in the previously mentioned doctrine that practical considerations like economic, technical and functional requirements should alone determine the design of the built environment. Nonetheless, an architect does need extensive knowledge of the various disciplines to be able to critically review, for example, improper construction methods. It is the challenge of being a teacher, as well as an art to convey all this knowledge, and to respect its importance, without inhibiting the design process.

For tutoring to succeed, the teacher should be able to switch between thoughts and emotions, between the abstract and the practical, synchronized with the student's increasing understanding of the assignment. Always alternate between the overview and the close-up view, since both the comprehensive level and the detailed level can provide important keys to a solution. It is a question of different scales, but in addition, it involves a mental proximity to the task: an ability to both concentrate intensively on details and to look calmly at the bigger picture. This process develops the students' skill in looking critically at their own sketch proposals (improving the ability to guess) and in making choices based on their own subjective/objective evaluations of the situation. For that reason, it is better for the teacher to show interest if a student has a divergent way of thinking, than to just be tolerant of it.

A difficulty in teaching is the balance between encouraging playfulness in creative work and the desire to seek new knowledge, while at the same time activating the student's own critical perspective. There are also situations when the student's overly strict critical perspective has to be controlled so that it doesn't lead to a fear of decision-making during design work. In these situations, a colleague of mine used to say: *try to like your proposal for a day or two, it's not forever. Then you're free to do something else.*

The teacher needs to have the capacity to look for new ways to understand the student's personality, because an inability to understand on the part of the student can be due to some problem with the teacher's instructions, or lack of them. One student may need challenges; another, careful suggestions. Donald Schön thinks that instructions are always incomplete and that the student can see them as ambiguous, strange, or contrary to their own perception of the situation. Every individual has to be approached in a way that takes into consideration his or her particular abilities and special way of thinking. With the goal of stimulating creativity, a teacher should reinforce the student's belief in their own ideas and help demonstrate how they can be developed. The situation is risky and challenging for the teacher also, as illustrated by the Norwegian Professor of Architecture Beate Hølmebakk:

> *As a teacher, I think you have to be subjective; express yourself openly, and you should be able to ask the same from the students who are willing to do so. When that vulnerability is lacking in the teaching situation, I believe the communication loses its credibility…*
>
> *… to practice our profession you need both practical and theoretical insight and competence, but to create really interesting projects, you need the skill of independent problem formulation and problem-solving. This independence is a pre-requisite for originality…and the capacity for critical thinking is one of the most important aspects to instill in the students.*
> (Psykoanalytisk Tid/Skrift 2009: *Om lärandet*)

It is always difficult to say what the student has learned (and not learned) from the experience of reflection during practical training, according to Donald Schön:

> *A practicum is a virtual world… it may fail because its striving for realism overloads students with practical constraints or…*

One of two fishing bridges on Myrbærholmen, Norway, 2010,
designed by Beate Hølmebakk and Per Tamsen (Manthey Kula
Architects) in response to the excellent fishing at that location.
Part of the Norwegian "National Tourist Routes" project. The
bridges are constructed of prefab galvanized steel segments,
cantilevering out 12 meters above the water.
Photo: Beate Hølmebakk

it leaves out too many important features of real world practice....
In order to be credible and legitimate, a practicum must become a
world with its own culture, including its own language, norms
and rituals. Otherwise, it may be overwhelmed by the academic
and professional cultures that surround it. (Schön 1990, 170)

The teacher must have a broad architectural education to cope with the whole spectrum of questions that are relevant to a student's proposal. Depending on which phase a project is at, it can involve everything in the area of *firmitas, utilitas, venustas*; for example, the exterior spaces, the intangible sensory values, traffic flow, vegetation, and other factors that help interpret the building site. There may also be issues of drainage, ventilation principles, or other technical aspects with the building. A teacher has to be able to relate these questions to the actual project situation, the student's skills level and his or her interests, and to be able to raise these issues at the right time.

On the one hand, the teacher needs to move the students into the realm of uncertainty so that they understand that the project can be approached in many ways and that therefore, many preliminary solutions have to be investigated. On the other hand, the teacher has to impart the courage to choose between these possibilities and to make decisions, while strengthening the students' confidence in their own decision-making. Many teachers in contemporary architecture schools describe design as a process of eliminating obstacles, and therefore they emphasize functional requirements, which may simultaneously restrict the students' ideas and conceptions. But at the same time, they talk about design as a creative activity; they emphasize personal expression, and worry about having too many restrictions. Mark Gelernter points out that building costs, which are a fundamental design restriction, are almost never mentioned in design studio education and building codes are either entirely ignored, or followed only if they don't collide with the primary design concept. Even when the teachers start the project by saying that satisfying the brief will be important for the evaluation, the highest grades are usually given to the most original proposals, despite the fact that they may not fulfill the requirements of the brief. According to Gelernter, the students are aware of this paradox because it is often part of the teacher's concept of design:

> *the challenge is to invent a workable marriage of applied*
> *science and artistry, classroom teaching and reflective practicum....*
> *Coaches must be first-class faculty members, and criteria*
> *for recruiting, hiring, promotion and tenure must reflect*
> *this priority.* (Schön 1990, 171)

Educating architects means that teachers also have to challenge their own creativity, so they need the freedom to create assignments, within the framework of the curriculum, that spark the students' imaginations. To react constructively to the students' proposals, the teachers must be receptive, be able to explain their method and tacit knowledge explicitly, and continually update their competence. It gives satisfaction when you succeed as a teacher in stimulating your students in their own way of thinking. A good teacher develops through the process of educating others, which could be one of the reasons that most teachers are very committed and devoted to their work, despite any possible difficulties. So how would you describe a good teacher of architecture? A student at Chalmers University of Technology in Gothenburg gave the answer:

> *Someone who conveys knowledge with humor and clarity, is not*
> *too serious, and [provides] actual tools. For example, a tutor once*
> *said: "Stop thinking so damn much, just get started."* (Wingård 2004/2005, 45)

Critics

Critics are generally architects who have not been involved at an earlier stage for the projects under review. Most often they are distinguished practitioners with their own architectural firms, preferably with some experience in teaching. Other critics may be academics with professional experience and theoretical insights. The group of critics should cover a wide range of knowledge. Architecture schools prefer to make use of well-known architects as critics, since this is seen to be a way to gain respectability when surrounded by university faculties that have high scientific standards. Arranging for the critics to give lectures in conjunction with their project reviews can also be a way to compete with other architecture schools. Structural engineers will often have their own reviews of the proposals, but occasionally, selected specialists from other disciplines will also be invited to a single review.

Critics may have a variety of viewpoints on the primary purpose of criticism, they can have different perceptions of their role, and they can be unaware of which type of criticism they use (see Chapter 7). Usually, the presented proposal is seen as the main object for criticism, while the process leading up to it is given less attention. The criticism can emphasize the proposal's architectonic qualities and tolerate weaknesses in building techniques, or it can do the opposite; concentrate primarily on whether the project is buildable, and if the mechanical equipment, details and costs are appropriate (i.e. normative criticism). One other interpretation is that the assessment reviews mainly serve the purpose of training for the student in preparation for presenting proposals to future clients.

All of these interpretations have educational potential, even if it is expressed in different ways. However, since the architect's *flexible thinking* and *ability to search for knowledge* are at the foundation of the profession, an emphasis on the design process is warranted as part of an architectural education. When the assessment review is also used for grading purposes, the situation becomes more difficult. The architect Sue Hall Jones (1996) described experiments done by J.B. Lowe which showed how critics' values affected their judgment. Lowe formulated a number of external factors that could influence the critics and their viewpoints and lead to different varieties of criticism. He made sure that most of these factors and distractions, for example, differences in lighting and thermal comfort, could be eliminated so that he could observe the review process more clearly.

The same people acted as critics in all of the experiments. The evaluation of seven proposals was done behind closed doors, without students. Lowe verified that the seven submitted proposals were redrawn with the same drafting tools, materials and conventions. Eliminating the students' variation in presentation techniques led to the most interesting results. A large number of evaluations were done, and it became clear that critics were not capable of making relative evaluations of the proposals when they were unable to use differences in the presentations in their criticism. The assessments were illogical, and by doing side-by-side comparisons it was shown that a single proposal could be judged *both* better and worse than another proposal. However, in general, Lowe's tests revealed the subjectivity of the evaluations.

The educational purpose of criticism is, at least for the lower years, to initiate a discussion that will help students increase their understanding of the *analysis through synthesis* method, make the use of certain concepts familiar, and also to discuss values, which gives awareness of the importance of architecture and strengthens the role of the architect. Unfortunately, talented practitioners are not always good at teaching, and good teachers are not always experienced enough as practitioners. According to Frank Weiner (2005), there have been successful, famous architects who have been great teachers, for instance: Mies van der Rohe, Louis Kahn, Carlo Scarpa and Herman Hertzberger (despite Mies van der Rohe being criticized for his character). Nonetheless, the combination of talent in both practical design and in the ability to teach is rare.

A critic who misinterprets their role can ruin the pedagogic goals of an assessment review. In Anthony's study (see Chapter 7), students spoke about critics who mainly wanted to manifest their own egos. Occasionally, critics could also engage in open conflicts with each other. Students often had negative opinions of critics and their way of criticizing the proposals, but no general conclusions can be made based on this material, since even relatively wide-ranging studies involve specific students, specific situations and specific criteria. We don't know if any other variables could be at play: why some students didn't answer the questionnaire; did they have something in common, etc. Assessment reviews at the same school can sometimes succeed and sometimes fail in utilizing the potential of criticism as a teaching tool. As stated earlier, numerous factors can contribute to this, but the most decisive factor is the performance of the critic, which is dependent on his or her professionalism, personality and pedagogical skill.

In addition, critics can have prejudices or preconceptions that affect their way of judging the presented proposal. Wayne Attoe gives several historical examples of architects' preconceptions. For example, John Ruskin's conviction was that ornament was the principal part of architecture; Bruno Zevi thought that architecture was mostly about space, not form or function, Nikolaus Pevsner emphasized the importance of national characteristics in architecture, etc. In a similar fashion, today's critics can have preferences or preconceptions based on their strong interest in, for example, sustainable buildings or the significance of sensory values, the Modernist doctrine of authenticity in building, or in performance-based architecture, created with digital techniques. All these starting points can be relatively easy to find and utilize for interesting and educational discussions, especially if the group of critics has different preconceptions. However, critics' perceptions of their own roles are harder to identify than their preconceptions.

Sometimes critics cannot resist the temptation to reinforce primarily their own self-identity, in order to establish themselves as the ones in authority over every question that comes up, and then refuse to accept any other interpretation than their own. In cases like this, it seems that they lack the ability to *distance themselves from their own egos*. Their need for self-promotion may be a trait of their creative personality, but it is a problematic quality which gets in the way of giving criticism. Critics may dislike a student because of his or her way of presenting a proposal. Such critics lack the ability to *distance themselves from their own feelings.* The strength of their self-confidence can be driven toward the weakness of arrogance. Being a critic requires solid integrity, but also sensitivity. Criticism is actually an art that can be performed more or less successfully.

The study that was mentioned earlier, done by Jeremy B. Lowe, included the finding that an important internal dynamic develops in a group of critics comprising two to four persons. He found that the jury members started their sessions with "*a polite but vigorous social confrontation*" which had the function of defining the status of the various members. Those with higher status could show their superior skills in criticism or ignore the opinions of the other critics. When a hierarchy had not been established there was a constant struggle for dominance, which influenced the judgment of the critics.[5]

The critic's self-identity, i.e. his or her interpretation of his own critical role, inherent prejudices and preconceptions, and the emotions at the time of the review are important. Disturbing factors like bad acoustics, or heat or cold in the room can influence the review. How the criticism is carried out can say more about the critics than the object or proposal that is being reviewed. This is exemplified and confirmed by the study results were described earlier which showed how an individual critic's behavior could be problematic. They could be overly self-aggrandizing or they could get into arguments with their fellow critics, and this could in turn affect the student who was presenting the proposal.

A further factor that can jeopardize the critique process is that the commentary by the critics is often improvised. Frequently, the initial questions and observations, even if relevant, are disparate or formulated in such a way that subsequent discussion is made more difficult. For example, in the case of a student's proposal for a spiritual space, the discussion was stifled by one critic's admonition that there is no need for any more religious spaces. This was in spite of the fact that the proposal was based on real needs from an active parish on an isolated island that lacked such a facility. The project was therefore realistic and endorsed by the client. Nevertheless, the jury member's severe introduction had a negative impact on the atmosphere of the entire review.

If there are too many ad hoc comments, the assessment review can become fragmented and the whole event can be unnecessarily difficult for the presenter. It may also mean that the audience has difficulty understanding the main problem in the proposal and the primary approach, thus eliminating the teaching potential of the review. It usually works much better if the critics (or one of them) try to comment initially (or summarize if the student has not done so) on the proposal's concept/primary generator—as it can be interpreted in the presentation. This puts more demands on the critics, but it provides a baseline for the discussions which ensue, so that if the student has additional clarifications, they can be placed in context. There are a great number of aspects that a critic can focus on. One of the most important is how well the proposal meets its goals as a result of intuitive and rational choices made during a well-executed *analysis through synthesis*. A discussion about the syntheses that were rejected on the path to a final solution can illustrate the level of the student's awareness and bring professional aspects of ethics into focus.

John Dewey summarizes the critic's task and position as the following:
> *That the critic must discover some unifying strand or pattern running through all details does not signify that he must himself produce an integral whole.* (Dewey 2005, 327)

The critic should not just replace the criticized work with his or her own. Comments like "It is a good (or bad) proposal" must always be followed by an explanation, even if very brief, or a reference to comparable projects. Otherwise, such comments are without substance, and they do not help the student or the audience to understand the problem.

It is a challenge to criticize proposals for buildings and environments because this demands that the critics quickly familiarize themselves with drawings and often, abstract models. Beyond that, a particular type of empathy is needed to be able to imagine the life that could be lived in the, as yet, unrealized environments.

The fundamental problem of analyzing the artistic impact of architecture lies in the fact that artistic quality can only be experienced and lived, and, consequently, the analysis of experience implies critical introspection. An architectural entity is so tightly bound by its artistic cohesion, the wholeness of experience, that it does not easily open up for rational dissection. (Pallasmaa 2005, 69)

Several students and former students who were interviewed by Parnell et al. (2007) had experiences of critics who were more interested in making an impression than in providing constructive criticism. Some students also encountered critics who were "worth their weight in gold". It is more difficult to say what it takes to be a good critic than what characterizes a bad one.

Critics can be inappropriate in their role when: they try to promote themselves in every situation; they cannot tolerate the slightest questioning of their authority, effectively smothering every attempt to start a discussion; they underestimate the students; they contribute clichés, or they neglect to study the students' proposals. If these traits are not restrained during the critique, they can undermine this valuable form of educational method that is specific to architecture.

A good critic is primarily deeply interested in the presented proposal and the student's way of thinking, "listens to the project", is receptive and acts constructively, when necessary. A good critic respects the independence of the students, their creativity and experiences, but is also involved, as John Dewey explains:

without natural sensitivity connected with an intense liking for certain subject-matters, a critic, having even a wide range of learning, will be so cold that there is no chance of penetrating the heart of a work of art. (Dewey 2005, 323)

Notes

References

1 Projective test method: a method that attempts, as well as possible, to use unstructured or ambiguous stimulus materials to exploit the human tendency to project their own experiences on the world around them (Nationalencyklopedin).

2 Scruton (1979), Bauman (1998, 41–43), Sudjic (2005), Silber (2007).

3 MacKinnon, D.W. from "Genius and Eminence" cited in http://change-log.ca/quote/2012/01/15/mackinnon_briefcase_syndrome_of_creativity

4 The study was done by Wayne Attoe from Louisiana State University and Robert Mugerauer from the University of Texas at Austin (Attoe and Mugerauer 1991).

5 The study focused on reviews behind closed doors, without students in attendance. Cited by Hall Jones (1996, 137).

Anthony, Kathryn H.: *Design Juries on Trial, the Renaissance of the Design Studio.* Van Nostrand Reinhold, New York 1991, 171–222

Attoe, Wayne: *Architecture and Critical Imagination.* Wiley & Sons Ltd. 1978, 5–8

Attoe, Wayne; Mugerauer, Robert: *Excellent Studio Teaching in Architecture.* Studies in Higher Education, Vol. 16, No. 1, 1991

Bauman, Zygmunt: *Globalization. The Human Consequences.* Polity Press 1998, 41–43

Blake, Peter: *The Master Builders.* Victor Gollancz Ltd. London, 1960

Dewey, John: *Art as Experience.* A Perigee Book 2005 (1934), 323–327

Dorst, Kees: *Understanding Design.* Gingko Press 2006, 99

Gelernter, Mark: *Sources of Architectural Form: a Critical History of Western Design Theory.* Manchester University Press 1995, 26

Graham, Elizabeth Marie: *Studio Design Critique: Student and Faculty Expectations and Reality.* A thesis. The School of Landscape Architecture. Christian Brothers University 2003, 36

Hall Jones, Sue: *Crits—An Examination.* Journal of Art and Design Education, Vol. 4, 1996, 133–141

Lawson, Bryan: *How Designers Think. The Design Process Demystified.* Architectural Press 2008, 151–158

MacFarlane Smith, Ian: *Spatial Ability. Its Educational and Social Significance.* University of London Press Ltd. 1964, 321, 330

Pallasmaa, Juhani: *Eye, Hand, Head and Heart—Conceptual Knowledge and Tacit Wisdom in Architecture.* In: Villner, L. and Abarkan, A. (eds): *The Four Faces of Architecture—On The Dynamics of Architectural Knowledge.* School of Architecture, The Royal Institute of Technology, Stockholm 2005, 69

Parnell, Rosie; Sara, Rachel with Doidge, Charles; Parsons, Mark: *The Crit: An Architecture Student's Handbook.* Elsevier Science & Technology Books 2007, 91

Psykoanalytisk Tid/Skrift 2009: 28–29 *Om lärandet* (On learning). In Swedish. Beate Hølmebakk in a conversation with Johan Linton, 319

Rand, Ayn: *The Fountainhead.* Centennial edn. Plume, New York 2005 (1943)

Romell, Dag: *Kreativitet—en outnyttjad resurs.* Hermods 1981 (1974)

Schön, Donald A.: *Educating the Reflective Practitioner. Toward a New Design for Teaching and Learning in the Professions.* Jossey Bass Publishers, San Francisco 1990 (1986), 105–111, 118, 170–171

Schoon, Ingrid: *Thesis. Creative Achievement in Architecture*: A Psychological Study, Leiden University 1992, 9, 15, 34–42

Scruton, Roger: *The Aesthetics of Architecture.* Methue & Co. Ltd., London 1979

Silber, John: *Architecture of the Absurd. How "Genius" Disfigured a Practical Art.* The Quantutuck Lane Press, New York 2007

Smith, Gudmund: *Mod att skapa* (Courage to create) In Swedish. Forskning & Framsteg 4/2000

Sudjic, Deyan: *The Edifice Complex. How the Rich and Powerful Shape the World.* The Penguin Press. New York 2005

Uluoglu, Belkis: *Design Knowledge Communicated in Studio Critiques.* Design Studies, Vol. 21, No. 1, January 2000, 38

Weiner, Frank: *Five Critical Horizons for Architectural Educators in an Age of Distraction.* European Association for Architectural Education. EAAE News Sheet 72/ 2005, 19

Wingård, Lisa: *Om att bli arkitekt.* Thesis. Chalmers School of Architecture, Gothenburg 2004/2005, 45

9 Assessment reviews: the presented proposal

To identify patterns in complexity: a review in year 2

The main character in an assessment review is neither the critic, no matter how skilled and cosmopolitan he or she is, nor the student, who is presenting the proposal. In fact, the real protagonist is the presented proposal. It speaks for itself when it is interpreted, commented on, criticized and (if) graded.

The way a proposal is presented and reviewed depends on the situation: for example, either as an assessment review in the lower or upper years, or for a client in a professional situation. Some of the following examples show which questions can surface in reviews in years 2 and 3, and the attitudes that the critics display.

In year 2, after an introductory course in building technology, all the students received the same assignment: to design a vacation cottage. The primary themes were: *materials*, *space* and *details*. The concept of *materials* was investigated during the project using specific partial assignments, field trips for the tutor groups, and a study trip for the entire group. *Details* relevant to the project were developed methodically through desk tutoring. Special focus was placed on the students' investigations and presentation of *space* and spatial relationships at different scales, from spaces in the landscape and exterior/interior relationships, to interior spaces and room sequences. The atmosphere created by physical constraints such as walls, floor, ceiling, light, materials, color, and their imaginary representation was emphasized. Life cycle analyses and technical aspects were also covered. There was a common comprehensive course description for the entire class which established the framework for specific courses and exercises arranged by each tutor group.

The student groups were mixed together during the final assessment review. The jury included an external critic, a structural engineer, and two teachers who had not previously been tutors. Practically all of the students started their obligatory verbal (approximately five minutes) presentation by explaining their project goals and the primary generator that was the impetus behind their proposal. For example, the great source of inspiration for one person was the *dialog between the mountain, the forest and the house*; for another it could be *isolation from neighbors*, or *spatial studies* (inspired by a Georg Perec text that they had read earlier); the concept of *vacation* was discuss-ed—*to get the feeling of vacation*; also *to overturn the conventional ideas of what a house is*. Other primary generators could be *contrasts in materials*, and concepts of *light/heavy*, among others.

Student critics had prepared questions to ask as soon as the student was done with their presentation. They asked about materials and lighting studies; what had guided the spatial organization and the lighting distribution. Occasionally a student critic would indicate, for example, that images from inside the house would be needed *"to see how you live in it"*. There were distinct critical comments, for instance, on minimal daylighting, or that a proposal was difficult to read. One proposal would be praised for excellent graphic presentation; another for facades with well-balanced proportions and a high level of detail. A student critic would suddenly exclaim: *"A concrete monolith in the middle of the forest is magical."*

The commentary and discussion revolved around the aspects that each proposal expressed. Hardly any of the proposals were evaluated completely based on *firmitas, utilitas and venustas*, but it was obvious after listening to the reviews of several proposals that the critics' comments made a more or less complete *pattern*, consisting of the criteria to be aware of in architectonic design.

The critics touched on and discussed a series of fundamental aspects, both as questions and as comments. They covered the following topics:

- *Placement on the site:* well-placed on the hill…exterior spaces, how you approach the site…sun, views…makes sense to build on a spot which would be otherwise uninteresting…sight lines…building on the ground versus elevated creates a different expression.
- *Massing and facades:* different principles for generating architectonic shapes and spaces were demonstrated: additive, by adding rooms together, or subtractive, where you create space within a larger form, in this case a cube.
- *Architectonic space:* …the corridor idea? A better solution would be a circular path, with no dead-ends!
- *Poetic expression and aspects:* …think about water and reflections when you work on the pool… the potential of terraces…the house being supported by columns is part of the architectonic expression—threatening, hovering… the feeling of warmth (brick) and cold (glass), etc.
- *Functional aspects:* …what are the minimum requirements? (don't be too conventional)…how do you use the house… talk about flexibility over time…spatial flexibility (sliding doors, for example)…nice bay windows with afternoon sun… why should the stove be movable?
- *Technical aspects:* we need to see solutions for moisture and condensation…water purification using a pool in the basement…building materials…cold or warm masonry walls… wood roofs, wood floors…sedum roofs, concrete walls.
- *Work methods:* when drafting digitally, you have to choose between a number of standard types, for example, railings. Don't choose until you know what you want!
- *Presentation:* beautiful graphically, but spatially ambiguous… fun using comics as an inspiration for describing life in the house.

There were occasional comments on how improvements could be made on plans or site placement, or how a roof should be detailed with the required insulation. Several students presented working models. In one case, a critic felt that an early conceptual model was clearly superior to the later model it developed into...*that was a disappointment.*

The assessment reviews were arranged in a traditional way, with the presenting student standing next to his or her presentation boards, which were hung on the wall. The critics sat at the front, with the group of students behind them, but this was not set in stone, since everyone took their chairs with them as they moved to the next presentation. The students who were present were active, participating several times with questions and comments on widely disparate aspects, for instance, possible detailing of roofs and eaves, various building materials, or *how much should you include on a site plan?*

Observing an assessment review in year 3

The intermediate review in year 3 had a different character. The students got to choose between four different assignments within the framework of their thesis project which they would present to the thesis jury approximately six weeks later. For the intermediate review, students from different groups were mixed such that three to four proposals for the same assignment were represented in each review group. A few days before the deadline, all the students received a schedule for the sessions. The review was called an *in-process review,* instead of an *intermediate critique* as in previous years, probably to avoid the general negative connotation of the word *critique*. It was clearly appropriate to try to assuage the students' anxiety and inspire them to work harder because, in contrast to their earlier projects, the thesis project was entirely graded. The goals for the in-process review were clearly defined. It should be based on constructive feedback that would illustrate the best qualities of the project and spark a discussion on how to develop them. Each proposal would be evaluated in terms of the course description, learning goals, and the teachers' outlines for the project. It was also considered very important that the students didn't just explain what they had done, but also described which issues they wanted to work with in the time remaining before the submittal deadline. Commentary would be provided on how these aspects could be further developed. One of the four assignment choices was to propose a renovation and adaptive reuse of their own workplace—the main building of the School of Architecture in Stockholm. This building, which has been very unpopular ever since it was opened in 1970, was seriously damaged by fire in 2011. The previous building on the site was originally built as a prison for women; then used later for the National Archives until the 1960s, when it was demolished. The new building which replaced it, to be used for the School of Architecture, was voted in 2008 by listeners of the Stockholm public radio station as by far the ugliest building in Stockholm. This may have something to do with the prison legacy of the site, but also with the building's particularly Brutalist style, which clashes harshly with the surrounding 19th-century traditional urban context. Despite its central location in Stockholm, the neighborhood is not very lively.

The building has a concrete frame with concrete masonry infill and the street facades are windowless concrete around a parking garage. A simple stairway leads to a mundane entrance on the second floor. The building is introverted in terms of turning its back to the city. The other side of the building, toward Engelbrekt Church, is more open, with a facade of copper, glass and wood above the lower section that was mostly destroyed by the fire in 2011. According to the Stockholm City Museum, the School of Architecture building has a significant cultural and historic value because, among other things, it has generated so many discussions and provoked so many emotions ever since it was built. Nonetheless, it faces an uncertain future, both because of the fire damage and a lack of maintenance, but also because a new building for the School of Architecture is under construction on the main campus.

The students were given a brief for the reuse of the building, to include housing and public space. The choice of these uses reflected a desire to vitalize the neighborhood.

School of Architecture, The Royal Institute of Technology. One of
the few Brutalist-style buildings in Stockholm. *Above:* The facade
facing the city. *Below:* The same buiding seen from the partially
fire-razed section. Photos: Carolina Krupinska

Seventeen students and two critics (A and B) who were teachers in that class (but not for those students) participated in the in-process review. One student kept time on a stopwatch: *"max. 5 minutes per presentation, 5 minutes of student criticism, and 15 minutes of assessment and discussion."* Each of the students presented their proposals in turn, and they were also scheduled to be an "opponent" for another student's proposal. The presented proposals were based on several diverse problem interpretations; for example, using the concept of *private, semi-private and public*, consciously reversing the introverted nature of the building, or focusing on the use of the spaces.

The author of Proposal no. 1 for the renovation of the building started with four principles: *urban remix, deconstruction/addition, embracing the city* ("because the building had been criticized for being a clenched fist") and *openness*. The student interpreted the brief to include student housing and offices. The goal was to:

> *separate the south wing, based on the site conditions, and introduce student apartments with direct daylight. Underneath the Triangle1 which now contains mechanical rooms, open up the circulation and bring in public activities in the lower floor wings…build a new addition toward the entry square with its own entry, in a public space…I haven't worked through the drawings very much; they don't really show what I want to do yet, but it's a first step.*

The student opponent was asked about the concept of *open/closed*:

> – *The concept of openness was important from the start, but I wanted to work with a discrete exterior. I realized that you would have to open up certain parts of the structural frame; the building is 10 meters wide, so you need a lot of daylight.*
> – *That's smart, but that image looks a little aggressive if you want to work with openness…. Have you thought any more about relationships with the surroundings? What about entrances?*

Another student joined the discussion:

> – *You've kept a lot of the exterior. People think the building is ugly,*

so considering the context, maybe it can become something else;
it might be time for a make-over.

Critic A returned to the student's introductory themes of embracing and hugging the city, and wondered *how* the building would accomplish that. After the student replied that it was *pretty basic, just open it up by removing concrete at the street level*, the critic went on to a technical question about presentations:

– *Is one of these models more accurate than the others;*
is there one that is final?… Parts of this presentation
are contradictory.

It was fairly obvious that the student had not decided which of the conceptual working models (his tentative syntheses) came the closest to meeting his criteria. Several problems were neither solved nor illustrated, which was pointed out by the critics. The student could often only give ambiguous answers:

– *How do you move through the building?…*
– *I think you come in underneath and then go up a stairway.*
– *So you walk through the building?*
– *Yes, exactly, there should be an entrance here, but I haven't*
solved it….
– *What about the courtyard? Is it public?*

Critic A noticed many unclear points in the presentation and repeated the question about circulation:

– *So if I arrive on bus number 2, I come in this way?*
Is it a public square or a park?
– *I haven't really defined it yet, but I want it to be open*
for housing, working, and pedestrians—and even have
a courtyard feeling.
– *That's a lot to study: cross-sections, models, the urban*
landscape, plus the building "hugging the city"…it will
be dictated by those constraints….If you carve things into
the facade, what happens to the infrastructure?

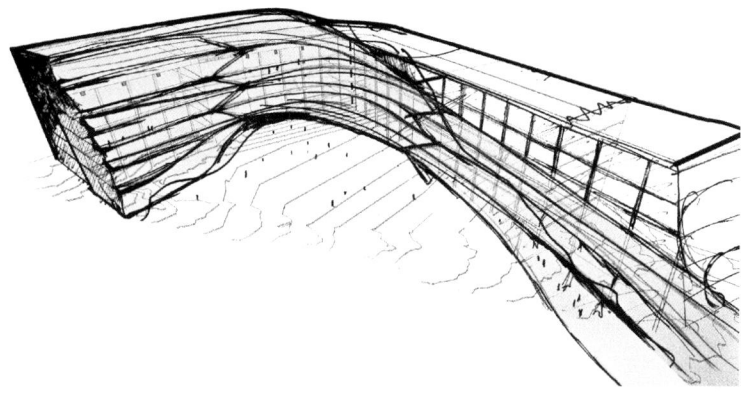

Proposal no. 1 was criticized in the intermediate review for
deficient investigation and evaluation, among other things (see
recorded interview). The above sketch shows an outline of the
proposed addition to the School of Architecture.
Photo and sketch: Dzenis Dzihic

Critic B balanced his comments between the contradictions inherent in the *analysis through synthesis* model: giving enough time to *search* for the necessary appropriate solution and then having enough time left to develop the proposal. He also clarified the individual and general aspects of the criticism by turning to the whole group of students and reading a few sentences from the explanation of the submittal requirements that the students had received well in advance of the review:

> *the EU directive states exactly the same thing. [It is a] government requirement to manage a project brief, complex problems, and relationships to surrounding buildings, which is why we have asked for a 1:400 scale site plan and the ground floor plan in 1:200. We didn't make that up. It's very important to be able to deal with the building site, housing values....Suddenly you start to understand things when you begin drawing them and you can decide how you handle the different spaces.*

He continued with comments on the presented proposal and he noted interesting thoughts that were worth developing, namely:

> *there is potential in connecting to this square [with] lots of sunlight... it can be the world's best place to hang around, but you have to develop the idea...you have to decide that your structure ends right here...it's not cheap, but (points out important economic factors)....It's a question of maximizing, to the max...*

Critic A asked:

> *– And what was the fun part of the project?*
> *– The actual search for the design.*
> *– Did you get stuck anywhere?*
> *–In the drafting process I drifted away from my original organic form...I've tried to create that form in a pragmatic way, then there are technical issues...the addition should express lightness.*
> *– A big model would help explain the different functions. You can be very free in a model, testing things. Structure and principles become apparent, and you think about materials.*

Critic B turned once again to the whole group with a challenge to attack different levels by drawing sections, reflecting on them (and redrawing as necessary). He finished the review with the words:

Basically, don't be fearful....You start thinking as soon as you start drawing. (See Proposal no. 1 being extensively reworked on next page.)

The student who presented Proposal no. 2 revealed a real entrepreneurial spirit. Her strategy was different than the first presenter. She had thought about economic and maintenance issues and she wanted to deconstruct the despised building by:

creating a sight line, a passage that is a natural short cut, but that also creates an entrance to the building. It will be a slice that brings movement into the building...I want to keep most of the concrete—the bearing structure—but add translucent materials, mostly along the lines of circulation...I want to create short-term housing that you can rent for a maximum of three years and other work spaces in the building....The floor plans get divided into a grid (3x3 m) and then you can lease the square meters that you need....After a while, you can evaluate the businesses to see if the leases should be extended...if there are those who rent living space and then start a business, they can get a lower rent...if you rent a work space, you can sleep there, too.

The student opponent:

- *It's good you have an idea of how it can work, that's nice with the small businesses, more activity.... The passage is very straight, maybe it should turn a bit [but] I understand your idea of being able to look straight through. What sort of businesses would be on the passageway?*
- *...you avoid the problem of removing the concrete...[what is] the infill material in the facade?*
- *That depends; I'm not sure...translucent materials and concrete.*
- *The materiality of the concrete is actually illustrated really well on one of the drawings.*

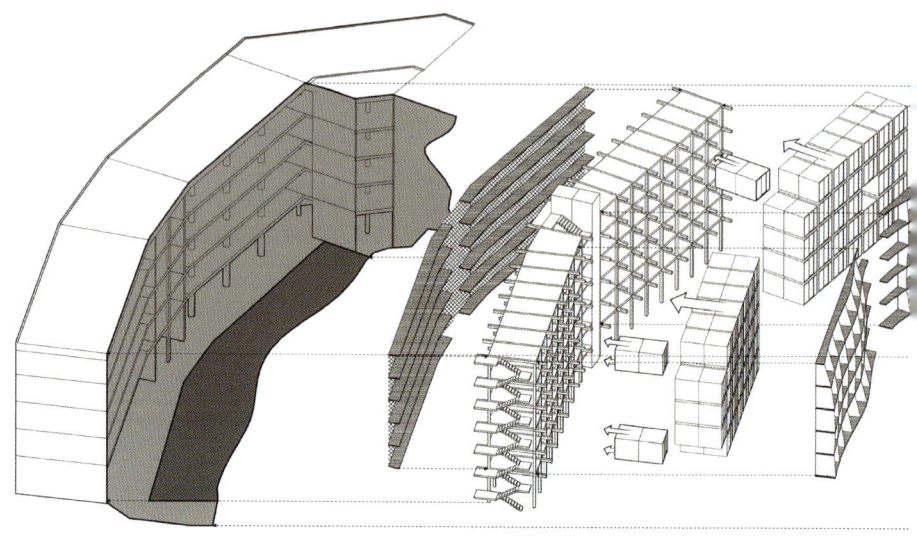

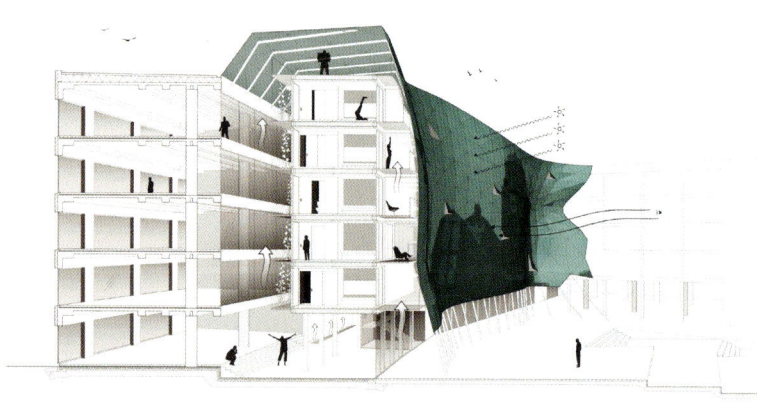

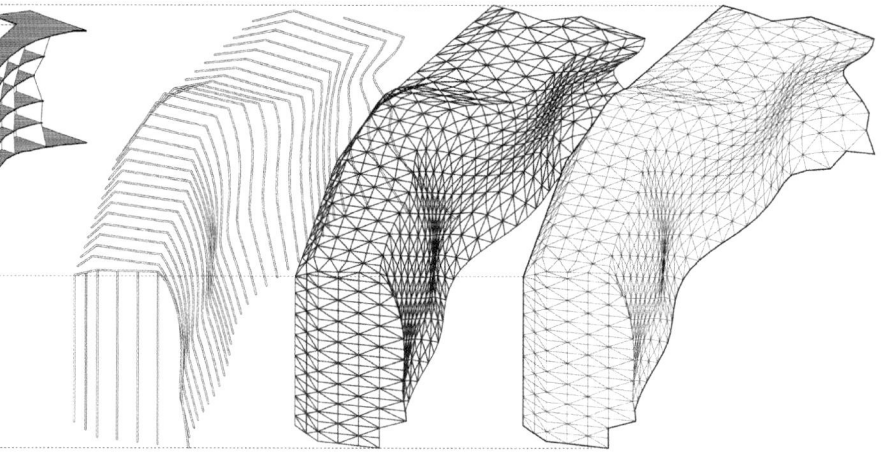

Above: Proposal no.1—extensively reworked—was presented
for the undergraduate degree and it received very high grades from
the jury. The massing studies above show how the added structure,
mainly constructed of glass and steel, connects to the existing
concrete structure. An atrium, enveloped by vegetation, is formed
between the "old" and the "new", transitioning into the access
balcony for the student apartments.

Left: The facade (skin), which can be opened, protects against
weather, sun and noise, and also generates energy—via photo-
voltaic panels that distribute power throughout the building.
Renderings by Dzenis Dzihic

Critic B wondered what the 3x3 meter units represented and if they were applied to both the housing and the office and commercial spaces. It is an extremely interesting idea to approach the project as an entrepreneur and use marketing principles to generate plan layouts and the appropriate architectural expression. The proposal investigated minimum space requirements and demonstrated unconventional thinking. Critic B also wanted to know how the student imagined life in the building, including practical necessities.

- *Now you have to tell us the advantage with the guiding principle, it doesn't have to be traditional housing....*
- *It's a despised building now, that's the reason to move through it...it feels natural....That also generates a new rhythm in the building.*
- *And is the slice coordinated with the structure?*
- *Yes, it is inside the concrete columns; you connect the steel to the concrete structure.*
- *Perhaps you should study what the slice looks like now or if you should change the form with angles. It is like a welcoming bridge to walk through, that doesn't have to be governed by structural factors. I'd recommend studying the spaces....You have to decide...so you can create spaces that match your wishes. Now it's kind of in the middle.*

The concept of time emerged in terms of the atmosphere in the passageway during day and night, which brought up the questions of lighting and the choice of translucent materials:

- *There are free solutions in your project, original ideas... it's very fun, but you have to have a lot of extra information to understand your vision and your system....*
- *Yes, I mustn't forget that you aren't inside my brain when I work, so my documents have to show what I want to do.*

Critic B encouraged all the students to take risks and use the freedom to experiment that you have at school. Also that the presenting student should make more definite choices, and:

– find the ultimate solutions, say what you want to do.
– It's hard to make decisions.
– But we are at a school.… You students should not be afraid to
   fail, you should take risks and try and next time it will be OK,
   you've learned, and you can do something else…you can speculate.
   When you get out, you have very little opportunity to speculate,
   you have to make decisions based on a lot of data. I understand
   your thinking, but at the same time, if you don't lock in some
   parameters quickly, you can't delve any deeper.…
– You probably already know (says critic A) *that you won't be*
   able to solve this situation for everyone, so you either have to
   make it very personal or you can think of a specific person that
   you can help with their housing needs. It is easier to be precise
   if the assignment is more constrained…I would choose some-
   thing; personal commitment or a particular person or group
   who needs a housing solution…imagine different scenarios.

Critic B also raised the question of the unique versus the general:
   Yes, that kind of solution will never satisfy everyone; 80 to 90
   percent of the people in Stockholm would never want to live in it,
   but that leaves 10 percent, or perhaps 100,000 or 200,000, who
   would. So base it on them and not on 2 million people.

The student didn't have any questions that she had been pondering
or that she needed help with.
   I can't think of any, but maybe I should do some scenarios?

All of the comments during the in-process review were directed at
the projects. The presented proposals were the main actors, not the
students or the critics. There were no negative statements like the
ones mentioned in Anthony's study (that applies to all of the proposals that were presented that day) and the critics were entirely
focused on the projects; there was nothing said about the students'
personalities or attitudes. The critics did not try to boost their own
egos either; they were simply good teachers.

Structure and criteria

Evaluating subject knowledge is not the primary goal of an assessment review. A traditional exam is better for that purpose. In contrast, an assessment review can demonstrate the student's ability to apply various skills and knowledge from different fields. The criteria that are used to judge an architectural proposal are derived from specific humanistic, technical and artistic fields, but standards from one area have to be coordinated with standards from another. For example, seen from a humanistic perspective, it can be important to point out that historical preservation can conflict with people's desire for convenience (old buildings may be cold and damp, but difficult to insulate) or with different uses for a building (problems with installation of an elevator, for instance), etc. Respecting the historical legacy can also require special structural modifications, resulting in economic considerations. Another complication is that the included parts may be seen as static or dynamic as defined by Attoe (see Chapter 7). Such conflicts between opposing demands are often very apparent in restoration projects, but they can, in fact, occur in any design work.

In the earlier description of the assessment review in year 2, among the seemingly random viewpoints, you will discover that the following overall checklist was used for the discussions:

- concept (or primary generator or guiding principle)[2]
- massing design and facades
- site layout
- the architectonic space
- poetic aspects and expression
- functional aspects
- technical aspects
- working method
- presentation.

For each point, different criteria were discussed in relation to that particular proposal. Some of the criteria were general, like those which should always be considered, i.e. concept, massing, spatial organization or approach. Others might only need attention in the specific proposal being evaluated, but *could be* equally important to consider in most other situations, for example: *exterior spaces, sun, views, makes sense to build on a spot which would be otherwise uninteresting, …* etc.

The account of the review in year 3, once again describing a rather unstructured discussion, reveals the same checklist—however, not explicitly, but as something already well known and unwritten, like a vocabulary:

- *concept:* private, semi-private, public
- *massing design and facades:* new addition toward the square, new organization
- *site layout:* interior/exterior, relationship to surroundings
- *the architectonic space:* entrances, entry, main entry, open/closed, how you circulate through the building
- *poetic aspects and expression*: the meaning of light
- *functional aspects:* lighting, practical requirements
- *technical aspects:* hole-cutting in floor slabs, framework reused, sustainability aspects, building materials— translucent and concrete
- *working method:* suddenly you start learning when you start drawing references (searching)
- *presentation:* the scope of the material, clarity, sections and models.

You can see this as a clarification of the Vitruvian *firmitas, utilitas* and *venustas;* the building or environment should simply be durable, functional and beautiful.

In both the year 2 and year 3 reviews, the comprehensive checklist provided an outline that indicated *what* should generally be covered for each problem interpretation. This outline was then expanded with criteria that mostly explained *how* or *what* could be "right" in particular situations, i.e. that north light is desirable in an atelier but not on a terrace, or that it is sometimes more appropriate to create additive rooms rather than subtractive. A number of these criteria are fixed, such as standard technical requirements for fire safety regulations or structural demands. Other criteria need research and reflection during the *analysis through synthesis* process, because they are dynamic, and vary depending on the situation.

A relatively distinct structure like this allows for a broad overview of the problem, so it should be introduced and practiced during assessment reviews. The purpose is to train the students gradually to be their own critics.

Design involves making a broad overview, followed by a summation of the parts so that you create a whole, in accordance with a given structure or a given guiding principle. The process of summarizing has a symbolic significance because it gives meaning: it can be an important experience, an insight about the laws of nature, an understanding of the world and society, or an artistic impression.[3] The ability to make a broad overview and summarize is essential in a design process, but it can enrich the understanding of any situation. It is very critical in the architect's job of *coordinating* building processes, while respecting the past, present and future.

Values determine the viewpoint you choose in these overviews and summaries. This may include ethical considerations or moral criteria based on different world views. For example, during an assessment review of a thesis project, such a value-based discussion became completely dominant when it was apparent that the presented proposal for a football stadium required extensive bedrock blasting and removal. The student's dream when choosing the lofty site was that the audience would have a great view from the grandstands over the adjacent lake. The complicated logistics of circulation, including accessibility requirements, and architectonic design of seating, etc. was very well planned. Nonetheless, the jury discussion barely touched on anything other than the inappropriateness of blasting bedrock, since particularly one member of the jury was upset that environmental values had not been respected.

As mentioned earlier, criticism can be more or less focused on product or process. In product-oriented criticism, the criteria are formulated as if the proposed building or environment was already built. You can concentrate on different aspects of durability, utility and aesthetics; for example, construction, environmental aspects, exterior/interior, logistics, functional solutions, optimal choice of materials in terms of costs, maintenance and aesthetics; details, but also "appropriate" massing, spatial solutions, lighting and color.

The path to the final solution can be straight or tortuous, depending on the students' interests and experiences, and the type of assignment. With process-oriented criticism, the focus is on the reflections that led to the various choices on the path to the final formulation. The questions that are asked include *how you got there* and can cover the following:

- the choices made and the motivation behind them
- considerations about the desired architectonic expression versus the result
- considerations on a general level concerning, for example, societal cultural conditions
- possible media interest, connection to contemporary movements, trends, interesting references.

The students are encouraged to take risks, which by definition means that they can sometimes fail. During your studies you learn from mistakes as well as successful proposals, as described in the earlier observations from the assessment reviews in year 3.

Incidentally, it may be said that the author of Proposal no. 1 felt a few months later that the intermediate review worked like a wake-up call, for instance, by offering the comment that producing drawings makes you simultaneously discover new things and learn more about your project. *"In my earlier naiveté, I had thought of drawings as presentation materials, not as tools for developing my project."*

Discussing process-oriented aspects has great pedagogical value at all levels of architectural education, as a way of reinforcing the students' awareness of how architects utilize their specific working method analysis through synthesis and architects' specific flexible way of thinking—the foundation of this method.

To grade or not to grade

As stated earlier, grading produces external motivation in students, and this can damage the teaching goals of assessment reviews, since it is primarily internal motivation that is a prerequisite for individual development.

Numerous studies indicate that formative and summative assessments[4] should be done separately and that anonymity is the only way to achieve that. Unfortunately, the anonymity that can be applied to various types of tests cannot be obtained when evaluating design, because it is easy to identify the work of individual students. If students know that the same people who are tutoring them will be deciding their grades, it is easy to suspect that a certain amount of opportunism will sneak its way into the teaching situation. Students can try to satisfy the teacher's values instead of challenging their own independence. The aforementioned study by Jeremy Lowe resulted in the conclusion that evaluations of student design projects are influenced by many factors that have nothing to do with the qualities of the presented proposal. The use of external critics is an attempt to avoid this problem.

Grading in design courses probably has more to do with ingrained academic routines than with good teaching practice. Despite that, a standardized grading system for architectural education in the EU countries was proposed around 2005. This standardization of grading systems was seen to be necessary because there was a great variety of grading scales, for instance, from 1 to 5 or from 1 to 30. In Germany and Austria, for example, grade 5 was a failing grade, but in Poland, grade 5 was the highest grade. In Portugal and Belgium, a grade of 20 was excellent, while in Italy it was barely satisfactory. There was not even any across-the-board standardization of grades in the Scandinavian countries. The range from low to high was minus 3 to 13 in Denmark, 1 to 3 in Finland, and in Norway F to A. Some architecture schools in Europe (mostly in Germany and France) required that their exchange students in Sweden be graded on a numeric scale, which was difficult because Sweden was only using descriptive grades: failed, passed, and passed with distinction.

The grading scale that has been proposed to be used throughout the EU is based on the letters A to F, where A is excellent and F is fail. This is not, however, without controversy. For example, The Royal Danish Academy of Fine Arts Architecture School in Copenhagen accepted the A–F grades initially, but then reverted to their original minus 3–13 scale after a short period.[5]

At certain architecture schools in Europe, graded assessments are used in most subjects and projects. At others, however, they are only used for thesis projects and some courses for the bachelor's degree (for example, at Chalmers School of Architecture in Gothenburg) while in Stockholm, they are used for the graduate architecture degree. In the new grading system, a proposal deserves an A grade when it is *an exceptional achievement that is clearly noteworthy. It shows a high level of independence.*[6]

Measuring knowledge and skills with graded assessments presupposes that such knowledge is measureable, which is not always the case. Measurements may be applied to scientifically based subjects like building technology or architectural history, where you can utilize tests and exams to reinforce the students' knowledge and help them develop competence in their design work. This kind of review of knowledge can also give students a certain feeling of security when they are confronted by the usual uncertainties in the design process. Grading skills such as freehand drawing, sculpture, digital techniques or verbal communication, etc. is more difficult than grading scientific knowledge, but perhaps it is possible. You may be able to assess ability, expertise, proficiency, talent, dexterity and artistic ability, but this involves a much higher degree of subjectivity than for scientifically based disciplines.

But it is doubtful whether it is beneficial or meaningful to have any comprehensive grades in design education. First, it is a dilemma to decide what should be graded: the presented product, as a summary of all of the included knowledge and skills, or the student's mastery of the *analysis through synthesis* method, as reflected in their presented proposal? These two elements rarely deserve the same grade. When you just look at the product, it is difficult to see if, and to what extent, it is a result of an independent and flexible thought process or the less thoughtful reliance on an example from an architectural magazine, for instance. The assessment is even harder if a proposal shows an excellent idea (primary generator), but weak construction solutions, or vice versa. What grade should the previously mentioned proposal for a football stadium receive if the student solved the complexity of designing an arena, but with a solution that required an enormous excavation? Ignorance of technical construction requirements can make a building much more expensive than it need be. On the other hand, the most inexpensive solution can have serious shortcomings in terms of architectural design or function. The inability to choose the best synthesis out of the full range of possibilities can lead to faulty interpretations of the problem, and so on, since it involves a large number of decisions based on different value systems.

The diversity of the teachers' and critics' perceptions of design and the over-emphasis on expectations of originality can also make grading more difficult. One literature critic pointed out ironically, in an analysis of assessment grounds for literary works, that originality is simply that which the critic has not seen before.[7] This could also be said of architectural works.

The possible arguments in defense of graded assessments for design could be that they:
  - stimulate the students to work hard in order to get the highest possible grade
  - help to gauge the student's level if applying from other schools

to the graduate program, i.e. after an undergraduate degree
- assist an employer in evaluating job applicants
- make it possible to rank design schools.

Even if grading would stimulate students to work harder, however, it can also be damaging because of the power struggle that Thomas Dutton writes about. He said that students are reluctant to share their ideas during their creative periods: "because if you steal my idea you might get the A instead of me". Also, the landscape architecture students that were interviewed in Graham's study felt that they would be uncomfortable discussing other students' work freely, because it might have a negative influence on their own grades.

Grades are hardly of importance when transferring from one school to another, nor when applying for a job. In reality, you don't look at grades; you look carefully at portfolios when evaluating students who are competing for admission to a design school. The reason is that even if grades are supposed to be universal by definition, they are interpreted differently at different schools. In contrast, a portfolio review reveals both the individual's competence and the quality of the architecture school they attended. It is also an internationally accepted procedure that job applicants show their portfolio, since an interview and a review of the portfolio are the deciding factors. In other words, architectural offices have faith in their own evaluations of prospective candidates, while grades are not given much attention. The perception that develops in the profession about the standard of education at the various architecture schools is most often based on the success of individuals who have studied there and also on the general architectural climate of that country. It is not grades that determine whether Holland, Denmark, Spain or Switzerland is considered to have the most interesting architecture in Europe right now. The European Union's striving for standardization takes no consideration of the fact that complex artistic works cannot be evaluated through the simplifications of grading systems.

To summarize, it is difficult to see other advantages of grading complex architectural proposals (and they are always complex) than its merely being a way to sort and provide the national higher education administration with statistical data.

Suggestions for improvement

Several authors have remarked that today's criticism is generally spontaneous and they would therefore like to see a structure for assessment reviews.[8] They also give recommendations for how assessment reviews can be improved. A great number of their points coincide with a general movement toward *a tighter organization* of the whole assessment review process, which means that:
- submittal of proposals will be at least a day before the critique
- all students will get an equal amount of time for review of their proposals
- students should get training in verbal presentation and be encouraged to participate in the critics' discussion.

Improve conditions for the critic's participation:
- distribute a brief before the review and ask the critics to use constructive criticism
- establish criteria for a "good" achievement and require written individual evaluations
- have the critics try out different types of criticism and then have them ask the students which type they learned the most from.

Perhaps many of the above recommendations have already been implemented at many architecture schools since they are based on studies that were mostly done, as stated earlier, several years ago. Practically all of these points have become routine in Swedish schools. One additional point, however, that should be emphasized is that the number of proposals to be reviewed in one day should not be too large, since it is easy to lose concentration. The following points are recommendations for the critics:

- *Listen* to the students' verbal presentations and *see* the presentation materials.
- *Verbally* describe the intention of the student and their proposal, and your own perception of the proposal.
- *Analyze* the student's proposal with a focus on the relationship of the whole to the parts, but also on aspects related to the site, time and potential users, i.e. the cultural, social and environmental context.
- *Discuss* alternative solutions.
- *Interpret*—i.e. clarify the meaning of the proposal/ design based on the critic's own values and, possibly, give an emotional or intuitive response to the proposal.
- *Guide the student*—suggest possible paths for the student's future design decisions, because "the ends of criticism should be beginnings".
- *Evaluate/judge*, after the assessment review, without the student present. This is also an opportunity to discuss the verbal and written evaluations. (Graham 2003, 83-87)

Prior to my first participation as a critic, I formulated a few simple points, which have served me well over the years, as my own check-list. This list also includes thoughts on how the students arrived at their proposals:

- What? Where? If?
- The anatomy of the terrain—continuum, spaces
- Constraints
- Concept (see note 2)
- Spatial qualities/structure
- Style/symbolism
- Building materials, maintenance, acoustics, ventilation
- Detailing
- Presentation.

This was complemented by asking the students to get a sense of being physically in their own buildings or environments. The goal was not to comment on each point, but to keep them at hand and discuss the ones that were relevant to each proposal. Every critic has their own way of looking at and evaluating presentations. A school can create guidelines, but their interpretation and application in the review is up to the individual critic. The fundamental point is that critics show that they understand the student's way of working and that they respect the student's independence in choosing a primary generator.

Several experiments are underway into alternative varieties of critique at different universities.[9] There is talk of the need to shift from an individual public defense to "a more democratic debate and discourse". The proposals for alternative critiques that are mentioned have the following goals:

1 *To encourage greater student involvement* by, for example, having them act as critics in other classes or by asking them to guess what emotions their proposals would produce in other people.

2 *To demystify the jury* and reduce its dominance by, for instance, letting the studio tutors grade the proposals, not the jury.

3 *To shift the focus from individual projects to the design studio* by arranging exhibitions of student projects where the visitors can comment on the proposals.

4 *To achieve clarity in presentations* (both in drawings and verbally) by letting the critics study and then present the proposals. Alternatively, by having a teacher present the proposal to the jury after the student has first presented it to them.

5 *Discourage the legitimization of hierarchical social relationships* that are reinforced by tacit curricula, i.e. unwritten, implicit rules, which neither the students nor the teachers in the design studio are aware of.

At Lincoln University in New Zealand, Associate Professor Jacky Bowring leads special courses in design critique for students in landscape architecture. Her purpose is to formulate criteria that are easily understood, even by inexperienced critics. Bowring tries to combine Attoe's categories of criticism—normative, interpretive, and descriptive—and she has created a checklist with perspectives/aspects to aid in evaluating a proposal. These are: function, symbolism, clarity, politics and theoretical approach. At the same time, she realizes:

> *While this checklist might help demystify the nature of criticism, it also dumbs it down—critique is an art and not a science.* (Bowring 2000, 47)

It may be worthwhile testing different models for assessment reviews, but the application of some of them can be problematic. The desire to have greater student involvement in order to sharpen their judgment unfortunately conflicts with grading, for example. Organizational improvements are important, but in the final analysis it is the critic's skill as a teacher that determines if the assessment review succeeds in developing the students' awareness of the working method of an architect and their responsibilities in society.

Analyzing: aspects of power and transactional analysis

It is sometimes said that students have minimal influence on the events in an assessment review and that they are essentially powerless. Someone else chooses the critics and what aspects to cover. Rosie Parnell et al. address the students with the challenge: "*You need to take more control of your own learning.*" Previously, Thomas Dutton and others had asserted that that power relationships should be a central point in discussions about changing the principles of assessment reviews:

> *When the review is structured in the typical show-and-tell routine where students stand next to the wall and often get ripped by professors, this is an asymmetrical relation of power. There's no dialogue in relations of power that are asymmetrical, and if there's no dialogue, there's no learning.* (Dutton 1991, 94)

Power relationships during assessment reviews were the focus for an ethnographic study that was done at a British school of architecture, as described by Helena Webster (2007). The study identified certain special aspects of power, for instance, that the reviews were periodical, which gave them a status of being natural and legitimate, or that different stories reinforced myths. For example, it was said that Mies van der Rohe tore down student drawings at assessment reviews, which strengthened the myth that it was accepted practice, thus reinforcing the teacher's authority and the student's fear. Both students and teachers perceived external critics as bearers of the values of the architectural profession and that their criticism could legitimize or question the work of the design studio. The critics had the status of judges. Additional examples of the asymmetrical balance of power were: the spatial organization of the furnishings in the assessment room (with the critics in the front row), the right of the critics to judge the work of the entire studio, and their right to define the words that were used in the reviews. Sometimes critics could interrupt the student presentations with words such as: "wrong", "bad", "rubbish" or "incompetent". All of this bolsters the notion that the symbolic power of the critics and the powerlessness of the students is something real.

Power is actually a complicated concept that may be interpreted in various ways. It is used in different contexts with different meanings. In the field of political science, the theory is that:

> *power can be discerned by observing divergence from four*
> *fundamental rights that every person should have in their inter-*
> *action with other people: autonomy, free will, equal rights, and*
> *equal opportunity.* (Beckman 1987, 118–124)

It can be interesting to reflect on how one relates to this theory in assessment reviews. *Autonomy* in the sense of independence and self-determination is probably a character trait for all of the participants. Awareness of this should result in mutual respect, which is impossible if derogative judgments are interjected, as in the British study ("rubbish", etc.). *Free will* applies, but with certain conditions for the participants in the review (e.g. the students choose their studio or course, but then have to accept the rules and methodology that are in place). Nevertheless, a positive learning experience is based on a dialog, so it is appropriate to explain why the course is organized in a particular way, and then discuss how it can be most beneficial. Something that is rarely mentioned is that assessment reviews not only benefit students; the teachers also get an opportunity to expand their view of architecture. Even the external critics benefit, because experiencing the student projects can give them a fresh look at their profession, and also inspiration for new thoughts. Some external critics feel that they gain in status by performing at the university level. It is *equality*, however, that is the most difficult to achieve in a teaching situation, as long as the teacher has the right to grade the student's work, but not vice versa.

A power relationship means that a particular individual has the opportunity to force his or her will on someone else. An educational environment is special because there is a fundamental asymmetric relationship in the principle of teaching, namely that those with greater knowledge and understanding pass it on to those with less. It can therefore be valuable to discuss the concepts associated with power: *authority* and *responsibility*.

Teachers and external critics have authority because of their experience and knowledge. They also have responsibility for education. In the student interviews cited earlier there were hardly any complaints about the critic's or teacher's authority; they were often appreciated for their commitment in helping students gain knowledge and awareness. However, *anti-educational* or *arrogant behavior by critics* caused uncertainty or displeasure in several of the cited cases.

During the assessment reviews described earlier for years 2 and 3, the critics sat in the front, near the proposal, which was then presented by the student, who stood up next to their work. All of this may be seen as a practical arrangement, not a demonstration of power. The critics who had not seen the proposals earlier could avoid misunderstandings by having the drawings nearby. A few of the students were asked by a teacher if they wanted to present their proposals from their seats, but they preferred to stand, since they felt it was easier to talk to the group that way.

You can see that the actors—students and critics—who perform during an assessment review can take on different roles: as coach, advisor or parent, just as the teachers do in the design studio. In the assessment review from year 3, described earlier, the critics were inclined to act as coaches. The important point, however, was that the students would have time to develop and consolidate their ideas before the submittal deadline.

Through the years I could sometimes see a *parent/child* relationship develop during an assessment review, which was rarely noticed by the participants. In a situation like that, the scope for a constructive discussion is limited. Psychiatrist Thomas A. Harris states, in accordance with so-called Transactional Analysis, that all those who interact with other people have behavioral patterns that may be summarized by three *ego-states:* "parent", "adult" and "child". In any given situation, one of these states is dominant. These behavioral patterns mean that you may instinctively find yourself behaving as a controlling parent and treat your discussion partner as a subordinate child (who may or may not accept that role). The decision to adopt the attitude of parent, adult or child is taken early in life, but these often subconscious behavioral patterns can be altered because they are based on your own decisions. At any stage in your adult life, you can make a conscious resolution to throw out the old attitude and replace it with a new one. An equitable discussion develops when both parties adopt an "adult" attitude.

Critics may also look at the assessment review in a similar manner to the behavior of a dictatorial parent. A student may get stuck in the role of "child" and be unreceptive to viewpoints and criticism. Both critics and students should strive to maintain an adult attitude, which includes the awareness that the criticism is directed toward the presented proposal and not at the student.

In the assessment reviews described in this chapter, there seemed to be a mutual adult attitude. The students, especially those in year 2, had a *discussion* with the critics and did not consider their statements to be directives.

Students have the right to be autonomous in their way of thinking. Their critics' viewpoints may indeed seem faulty, so students must have the freedom to make their own choices and allow themselves to expose their uncertainties, with the overriding goal of learning. In the end, it is not the critic's comments that are the most important results of the assessment review; it is the reflections that are generated in the students, which stimulate their *learning*. Independence, creativity and self-confidence are reinforced as one's critical viewpoint develops, and judgments from others are of secondary importance. The ability to reflect critically on your own proposals helps you deal with uncertainties.

Martin Heidegger said that teaching is more difficult than learning, not because a teacher has to know considerably more than the student, but because a teacher must be able to teach the student *how to learn*.

> *The teacher must be capable of being more teachable than the apprentices. The teacher is far less sure of his material than those who learn are of theirs. If the relation between the teacher and the learners is genuine, therefore, there is never a place in it for the authority of the know-it-all or the authoritative sway of the official.* (Heidegger 1993, 380)

Notes

References

1 A large, existing, triangular hall that extends through all of the levels, in the part of the building that survived the fire.

2 Concept in the sense of an initial idea, but including its consequences. See the discussion of terms in Chapter 6, pp 142–146.

3 According to the German philosopher Cassirer's thoughts in Bundgård (2006, 42).

4 Formative evaluation focuses constructively on the project's development; summative evaluation focuses on grading.

5 The odd Danish grading scale is -3, 0, 2, 4, 7, 10, 12 where "passed" is from 2 upward.

6 According to an interpretation at The KTH, School of Architecture, Stockholm.

7 Anderberg 2009, 25.

8 Anthony 1987, Graham 2003, 88–89; Parnell et al. 2007, 136.

9 Anthony 1991, 120–137; Parnell et al. 117–128; Dutton 1991, 174.

Anderberg, Thomas: *Alla är vi kritiker. Om den nödvändiga konsten att värdera och kritikens osäkra grunder.* Atlas 2009

Anthony, Kathryn H.: *Design Juries on Trial, the Renaissance of the Design Studio*, Van Nostrand Reinhold, New York 1991, 120–137

Anthony, Kathryn H.: *Private Reactions to Public Criticism: Students, Faculty, and Practicing Architects State Their Views on Design Juries in Architectural Education.* Journal of Architectural Education, Vol. 40, No. 3, 1987, 2–11

Beckman, Svante: *Sorterad makt.* In Peterson, Olof (ed.): *Maktbegreppet.* Carlsson Bokförlag, Stockholm 1987.

Bowring, Jacky: *Increasing the Critical Mass: Emphasising Critique in Studio Teaching.* Landscape Review, 2000: Vol. 6, No. 2, 41–52

Bundgård, Peer F.: *Ernst Cassirer. Om kulturfænomenernes struktur og betydning* (The Structure and Meaning of Cultural Phenomena). In Danish. In: Thau, Carsten (red.): *Filosofi & Arkitektur.* Kunstakademiets Arkitektskole 2006, 42

Dutton, Thomas A.: *Architectural Education and Society: An Interview with J. Max Bond Jr.* In: Dutton, Thomas A. (ed.): *Voices in Architectural Education. Cultural Politics and Pedagogy.* Bergin & Garvey, New York 1991, 92–94

Graham, Elizabeth Marie: *Studio Design Critique: Student and Faculty Expectations and Reality.* A thesis. The School of Landscape Architecture. Christian Brothers University 2003, 81–89

Harris, Thomas A.: *I'm OK—You're OK.* Avon Books, New York 1973 (1969)

Heidegger, Martin: *Basic Writings from "Being and Time" (1927) to "The Task of Thinking" (1964).* Routledge, London 1993, 380

Parnell, Rosie; Sara, Rachel with Doidge, Charles; Parsons, Mark: *The Crit: An Architecture Student's Handbook.* Elsevier Science & Technology Books 2007, 114, 136

Thau, Carsten (red.): *Filosofi & Arkitektur* (Philosophy and Architecture). In Danish. Kunstakademiets Arkitektskole 2006

Webster, Helena: *The Analytics of Power. Re-presenting the Design Jury.* Journal of Architectural Education, Vol. 60, 2007

10 Awareness and understanding

Advanced-level criticism

For several years, within the framework of a so-called SOS Abitare project, the architectural magazine *Abitare* published an open invitation to architects to submit their recent projects for criticism by renowned architects. Several architects used this opportunity, and the magazine published critical reviews of a number of the proposals. In *Abitare*, No. 491 (2009), a proposal for a single-family house in Italy was presented. The brief was to design a "Mediterranean" house on a garden lot, which had a retaining wall separating it from a lower street. The lot was subdivided from a larger lot that was owned by the woman's father. The house was designed for a small family. The presented proposal consisted of two separate houses with separate entries, one of which was only the size of a guest cottage.

Rem Koolhaas and Renzo Piano acted as two independent critics, but their criticism was not presented concurrently, as in assessment reviews at architecture schools, but on two separate occasions. Koolhaas' criticism was in the form of a discussion with one of the designers, while Renzo Piano submitted his comments as a monologue.

Koolhaas felt that the main idea behind the proposal—separating the house into two parts—was not a convincing formula, considering conceptual aspects. He asked *why* and *for what gain,* and he argued instead for the use of psychological aspects and family relations as a basis for an alternative idea. He pointed out that interior rooms in the proposal were neither large nor small, neither closed nor open. The design did not utilize the opportunity to create architectonic qualities by differentiating spaces. Koolhaas also discussed the significance of scale and indicated that a small house is just as complex, hard to design, and equally important as a large one. While

questing the window design, he emphasized the value of a critical stance in relation to normative aspects:

*I really like Italy, but sometimes it's very difficult for me to
understand whether the things are where they are because
of considered choice or because there is an enormous amount
of things that have never been questioned.* (*Abitare* A 491)

In his criticism, Renzo Piano emphasized the importance of listening carefully to the client's "unspoken words" and establishing an
"extremely close relationship with your clients" in order to put your
finger precisely on what they need. Once again, these are the same
psychological factors that Koolhaas described, but expressed in different words. According to Piano, a sense of the character of the
place should determine the atmosphere and help define the emotions the building should evoke—which is essential, no matter what
object you are designing. Piano indicated in his critique of the
single-family house that the massive wall around the site could be
used to give character; it could be extended and the house could
grow out of it. He also mentioned the microclimate (sun and wind)
as another important element. The window design was discussed
briefly and beyond that, he hardly commented on the building
design at all.

In their relaxed and rambling commentary, both Koolhaas and
Piano considered the proposal's concept/primary generator to be
the most important aspect, even though they approached it from
different perspectives. They attempted to search for possible "architectonically active elements" when they could not find them in the
proposal. They saw the product, but at the same time they indicated
indirectly that there were deficiencies in the method, because
the presented proposal was not the most appropriate choice out of
several possible ones (the others had perhaps not been studied).
Koolhaas used dichotomies (large/small, closed/open, etc.) as a kind
of checklist that delineated various aspects of the proposal, but they
were discussed very briefly, presumably because of the limited space,
but also because it was uninteresting to start a deeper professional

discussion when the idea had not been convincingly chosen in the first place. However, in a teaching situation, there is pedagogical value in fully covering the main idea as well as other relevant aspects so that the students can gradually build up their own set of criteria. These criteria are helpful when making the decisions that have to be made at every level of design work. In discussions between experienced architects, the criteria are generally well established and self-evident.

There are several examples in *Abitare* of criticism of various proposals that follow a pattern similar to the one mentioned above. They demonstrate that the various critics can have completely different approaches and also they can focus on different things. For example, Junya Ishigami formulated his critique of a pre-school by creating a number of sketches, then investigating alternative placements for the building and their consequences in terms of play areas and possible gardens, etc. His criticism of the proposal resembles the guidance of a skilled tutor who is able to make quick sketches in the studio that open a world of possibilities for the students. In her criticism of the same proposal, Denise Scott Brown chose instead to concentrate on functional aspects and a sensibility for the need children have for exercise and play.

Risk-taking and choices

Both Rem Koolhaas and Renzo Piano directed their attention to finding a concept that could be applied to the smaller house. It is noteworthy that they (and even Ishigami and Scott Brown) focused initially on two fundamental aspects: first, considerations relating to empathy for the people involved; and second, dealing with the architectonic space, both interior and exterior. Their choices seemed solid, as a result of their skill, intuition and experience. It is precisely that ability, of instinctively reflecting on your own proposal, that you want to establish while training to be an architect.

Today you cannot rely on the experience and knowledge of craftspeople or style specialists. A student cannot observe a master/

teacher in practice, imitate them, be corrected, and gradually learn professional methods. In the design studio, the situation is almost reversed; it is the student who is producing solutions for a given problem; the teacher then reacts to them, and thus provides guidance for the *analysis through synthesis* method. It is rarely mentioned explicitly that the process of analysis through synthesis primarily involves *qualified guesses* where the answer to the inquiry should be multi-dimensional in the sense of time and space, and where several answers are possible. These guesses can gradually become more certain because the search for syntheses opens the door to new knowledge. An answer that initially seems correct can fail when tested. It may take a series of evaluations to find an appropriate solution. This process gives the student an opportunity to discover, together with the teacher, what kind of knowledge is needed. An extensive individualization of the teaching is necessary to demonstrate and instill the *analysis through synthesis* method with its sketch process and flexible thinking.

The word *guessing* can sound unprofessional and incompatible with the architect's academic status or with the culture of expertise that characterizes the architect's collaborators (engineers). It is therefore interesting to note that Karl Popper, one of the greatest science philosophers of the 1920s, maintained that scientific knowledge actually originates from guesses. He explained that scientists guess their way forward by producing daring theories which risk being disproven. The theories are then exposed to vigorous critical discussions and testing. This procedure has a strong resemblance to the architect's method, including flexible thinking, risk-taking, and the use of criticism as a tool to advance knowledge.

With the help of a successively greater skill and knowledge base in humanistic and technical subjects, the student finds that the range of possible solutions is expanding. Eventually a student can start projects with a much broader scope, just as experienced designers do. Knowledge that is built up progressively during architecture school and through later practical work provides a foundation that is complemented by experience. This applies both to the *explicit* knowledge that is theoretical, objective, easy to collect, comprehend and document, and the *implicit, tacit knowledge* that only belongs to the designer. *Tacit knowledge* is often unwritten, difficult to express in words, and sometimes the individual is not even aware of its existence. It is practical, based on experience, and is obtained through training and practice. It is part of the basis for decisions, but difficult to use for legitimizing them. It is knowledge that is gained by one's own attempts at *doing*.

The big step from a more or less vague idea—an imaginary image—to a proposal that is gradually more precisely defined is supported by several choices made during the sketching stage. *Choosing* involves risk-taking on numerous levels: the preparations can never be complete, the initial knowledge can hardly be comprehensive, the ability to sketch and produce presentations can be deficient, and there is no prepared solution to follow. Choosing the right problem formulation and a satisfactory concept are not the only decisions during the design process. Every step along the way involves several additional choices between aspects that deserve special attention; possible perspectives, ethical and aesthetic decisions, and often parallel choices on finalizing functional solutions, building materials and finishes, construction details, etc. This process is guided by subjective judgment, unarticulated tacit knowledge and intuition. Professional competency is primarily demonstrated by the ability *to choose*, according to Wittgenstein.

Changes in a proposal in progress can lead to several other revisions or possibly undermine the entire idea. Donald Schön's concept of reflection-in-action is relevant here. This is a way of training oneself in professional self-criticism. It would certainly be easier to make your choices based only on confirmed knowledge and then be able to prove the accuracy of your solutions, but the research cited earlier shows that both rational/objective and subjective values have to be weighed together in a complicated process. The ability to choose is central to working as an architect.

But would it be possible to avoid making choices? Is it not just random events that control the work of an architect? One student, who was working part-time in an architectural firm, wanted to test these questions in his thesis project. The task was to design a housing development on a site adjacent to a ferry terminal. The student's proposal for approaching the design process was as follows:

1 Every day for a year, draw a random, meaningless doodle on a copy of the site plan.
2 Interpret several of the doodles as three-dimensional plaster models.
3 Randomly choose a few of the three-dimensional plaster models for continued development.
4 Reinterpret these forms on a plan drawing.
5 Throw dice to determine the building heights in different parts of the plan; then adjust them according to sun studies and acoustic conditions.

This sounded unconventional and adventurous, but because of the student's previous solid work and experience, the outline for his experiment was approved. The doodles in step 1 eventually evolved into a thick book and he proceeded as planned. Finally the project was presented to a thesis jury, in front of a large audience. The excitement was palpable. One of the jury members, Professor Per Olaf Fjeld from the Oslo School of Architecture (AHO), turned the jury's initial uncertainty into a very interesting discussion on randomness and the choices you are faced with as an architect. The discussion resulted in the conclusion that despite all the random aspects of the presented work, several conscious and semi-conscious choices had been made. Chance can indeed steer the process to some extent, but the designer's judgment cannot be excluded. The rational choice that is idealized in the Western world, founded on Plato's idea that different alternative choices can be evaluated based on *a single* quantitative value standard, can hardly be utilized by architects. Maximizing one value to make one correct choice and simultaneously eliminating emotions to avoid irrationality is not

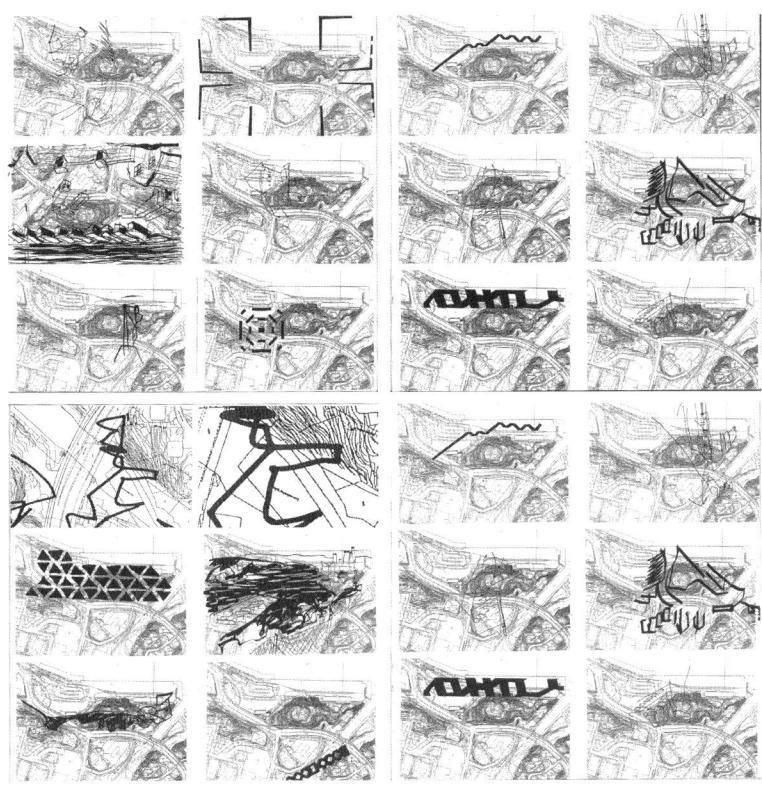

Is it not just random events that control the work of an architect?
"The Path of Randomness"—a thesis project by Anders Berg.

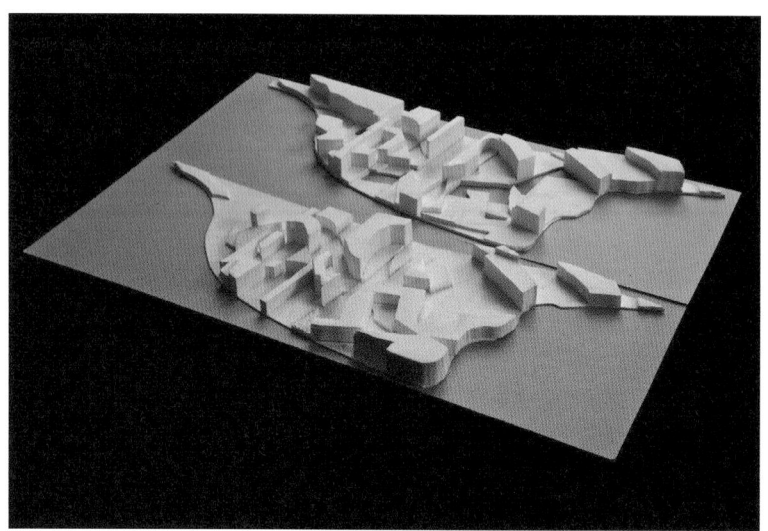

Examples of a few doodles transformed into three-dimensional plaster models. "The Path of Randomness" by Anders Berg.
Photo: Lennart Johansson

plausible. It is scarcely possible to meet such a demand, because there are so many qualitative and quantitative aspects that are important. The latter aspects can be governed by different measuring systems. Numbers and values you use in a single design can have entirely different meanings. Measuring quantities may be helpful in evaluations, but by itself it is not an evaluation method. A choice must rely much more on qualitative methods.

Expressing qualities in distinct terms is difficult, while it is easy to standardize something that is measurable. Standards can be attractive because they simplify verification, while checking qualitative values is harder. The quantitative values may thus become dominant, which is often evident in discussions with technical consultants. Nevertheless, it is the qualitative values that are more decisive for the outcome of a designer's work.

The ability of architects and other designers to make correct choices seems to rely more on Aristotle's way of thinking than on Plato's, according to Martha Nussbaum in her essay on rational choices. Plato wrote that the "art of measurement" leads to a rational choice, which could be included in a system of general rules, and then be applied to every new case. But Aristotle believed that the truly rational way to choose is to reflect on a complex situation, accept each part's specific character and utilize this understanding of the situation's heterogeneous nature as a central element in the decision. Practical insight involves the ability to "use reason in an improvised, hypothetical way". The nature of practical wisdom is that it can only be weakened by becoming more "scientific". Aristotle considered individual choice to be superior, both in accuracy and flexibility, and his thoughts actually describe the decision-making that characterizes a design process.

> He tells us that a person who makes each choice by appeal to
> some antecedent general principle held firm and inflexible for
> the occasion is like an architect who tries to use a straight ruler
> on the intricate curves of a fluted column. No real architect does
> this. Instead following the lead of the builders of Lesbos, he will

measure with a flexible strip of metal, the Lesbian Rule, that
"bends to the shape of the stone and is not fixed". (Nussbaum
1990, 69–70)

The right decision is like improvisation in drama or music; it requires flexibility, sensitivity and receptivity to your surroundings. Putting your faith in an algorithm is not only insufficient; it is also a sign of immaturity and weakness. Choice is defined as an activity on the boundary between intellect and emotion, deriving from both. People with practical wisdom reveal an emotional openness and sensibility when they encounter a new situation.

Designing as an architect involves the attempt to get an overview of the given problem, its possible interpretations and choices, but also the ability to reject inappropriate solutions:

In practice, therefore, the question is not so much "why does the
architect choose certain relationships of spaces" but rather "why
does he reject certain relationships of spaces?" The quality of an
architect's creative talent may well be measured by the variety
of spaces he is capable of conceiving; but the quality of his judg-
ment depends upon his criteria of rejection, and the scruples
with which they are applied. (Collins 1971, 41)

In any event, architects must allow themselves to think creatively before they start applying value judgments and rejecting choices. A subjective and objective evaluation of a proposal's advantages and disadvantages must be done, despite incomplete information and knowledge. The constant reflections that are part of the design process must be flexible so that the range of possible solutions does not shrink too quickly. It is often a question of having the ability to *delay judgment.*

Awareness and understanding

The choices that a designer makes are mostly dependent on values. It is values that let us become convinced, make decisions, and act despite uncertainty, but many of a designer's values are considered suspicious and unreliable in today's rational world.

> *It is frequently tempting to employ more accurate methods of measurement in design than the situation really deserves.... It is tempting to avoid these difficult problems of judgement by instituting standardised procedures....What a designer really needs is to have some feel for the meaning behind the numbers rather than precise methods of calculating them....It is thus more a matter of strategic decisions rather than careful calculations.* (Lawson 2008, 70–71)

It is a dilemma that the complexity and uncertainty, value conflicts, and complicated ethical aspects that are part of architectural practice cannot be solved through normative process models (it would be so much easier). In the end, it will always be the designer's task to decide on the value judgments that yield the best possible solution for a given situation.

You cannot look at architectural work without discussing the future, since built objects affect the future life of so many people. The values that influence this work are not just the private values of the architect; they have several ethical aspects. The role and responsibility of the architect requires a sensibility for current societal norms and an awareness of predominant values. The fundamental values that are emphasized depend on the contemporary paradigm in society and the architect's innate and learned emotional and social motives, political viewpoints, etc.

Many famous architectural works were created to demonstrate power or the immortality of those in power (e.g. the pyramids of Egypt), but also religious and political movements. There are numerous examples showing how some architects have had dubious collaboration with totalitarian regimes, as illustrated by the architectural theorist Dejan Sudjic in his book *The Edifice Complex. How the Rich and Powerful Shape the World* (2005). The actions and values of Le Corbusier and his radical plans for urban renewal are also questtioned by many critics.[1]

A lively discussion about the values that control architectural design continued for a number of years after the student revolts of 1968. Industrial designer Victor Papanek's influential book *Design for the Real World* (1971) and his statement that *Design should be moral* inspired the interest of many architects in environmentally conscious design and design for the poor. A well-known example of Papanek's designs is a radio for the third world that only needed a burning candle as its energy source.

An architect's values may be based on ethical and aesthetic grounds, as well as logical, sensory or pragmatic ones. For example, early in the 1960s, the architect, visionary and inventor R. Buckminster Fuller emphasized the importance of thinking globally. He was ahead of his time in evoking an awareness of global problems: climate change, environmental degradation, regions dominated by poverty, and global financial crises. He believed that through innovative thinking in the long and short term, individually and in collaboration, architects and designers could contribute to global change that would benefit humanity. He introduced the science of synergy, i.e. the study of systems with interacting factors where the result is greater than the sum of each different part. Based on these principles, he developed a series of ideas and innovations; the most famous being his light, self-bearing geodetic domes. He was also one of the first people to direct an interest into sun and wind energy. Fuller was decades ahead of his time, but despite his ability to advocate his ideas, the concepts of sustainability and resource conservation did not make a great impact on the architectural profession.

However, Ralph Erskine, working in Sweden, was also aware very early on of the possibility for an architect to have a political and social influence on the development of society. During his whole professional life, he had a great influence on the architectural debate, both in Sweden and internationally. Many architects began to work in a spirit of environmental and societal responsibility.[2] The publication of the UN report in the 1990s defining sustainable development as something that *satisfies today's needs without jeopardizing future generations' opportunities to satisfy their needs* contributed to increasing the interest in sustainability. The awareness of designers of the need to think globally, in the long term, without disciplinary boundaries, has gradually influenced architecture schools and, in many cases, the architectural profession.

Other dominant values may be discerned in sensual buildings designed by Peter Zumthor; for example, the Thermal Baths in Vals, Switzerland. Zumthor and other architects inspired by phenomenology emphasize the sensory aspect of the architectural experience: touching, seeing, hearing and smelling. Zumthor asked himself what it was that affected him in certain works of architecture and he realized that it was the building's material qualities and physical presence, but also light, silence, the tension between interior and exterior, context, and beautiful forms. He highlighted an issue of sensibility, where all of the senses are present and activated (Zumthor 2006). His perception of what architecture is and how we experience it influences his values.

> *The design process is based on a constant interplay of feeling and reason. The feelings, preferences, longings and desires that emerge and demand to be given a form must be controlled by critical powers of reasoning, but it is our feelings that tell us whether abstract considerations really ring true.* (Zumthor 1998, 20)

Thinking about sustainability and how architecture is experienced are actually two sides of the same coin, since both aspects are based on people and their position in ecological systems.

Many values are passed on in architectural education, but ethics is rarely part of the curriculum in European architectural schools. In North American universities, ethical issues first came to the fore when the teachers from the Bauhaus moved to the USA in the 1930s, but it was not until the 1970s that ethics was introduced as a subject in the architectural curriculum. However, ethics in the field of architecture is a complex issue, because of the architect's relationship to different groups that are involved in the design and building process, such as users, clients, politicians, bureaucrats, etc., and also due to his or her relationship to the architectural profession itself and to colleagues. Professor Thomas Fisher at the University of Minnesota College of Design has written several texts discussing how a deep understanding of ethics can help architects utilize their professional knowledge in an effective way to meet the current challenges that the world faces.

It is not easy to answer the questions *why* I do something, *what my decisions are based on, what is important in today's world and in the future*, but designers have to ask these questions in order to develop their professional awareness and find their role in the development of society. In addition, the designer may eventually be more convincing when presenting his or her decisions in front of others. The architect's gradually accumulated knowledge and skills, plus the mastery of the architect's working method, are important, but individual and group values actually determine how the final summary is done.

This is what requires reflection and awareness; how will architecture relate to the world of the future and how much can it change our world for the benefit of humanity?

Final words

Architecture can be *simultaneously* poetic and pragmatic, and the everyday work of the architect relies on both a theoretical and practical foundation. The field of architecture covers aspects from humanistic and scientific subjects, technology and art. To combine all of these ingredients, architectural education uses a teaching methodology with two basic goals. The first goal is to instill the ability to manage complexity with the *analysis through synthesis* method, which includes free and dynamic thinking, and is a prerequisite for a creative relationship to the outside world. The second goal is that students learn to condense *firmitas, utilitas and venustas*; not only each part, but as a whole—a beautiful, durable building or environment that focuses on people and their needs. To reach these goals, students must gradually build up their knowledge in humanistic and technical subjects. Audacity and playfulness must be encouraged, but also awareness of values—their own and others'. In addition, becoming an architect involves developing an instinct to constantly seek and learn; to know always that there can be other ways to interpret a problem and that there can be many possible solutions.

Criticism in the studio, assessment reviews, and the criticism that continually takes place in the architect's practical work, with approximations and risk-taking, is included in architectural education as a way of developing the students' ability to criticize their own work.

The use of dichotomies in sketching was described in Chapter 6. There are several dichotomies and dynamic conflicts that the architect must deal with on a daily basis. This demands constant shifts between emotion and reason, overview and detailed view, quantity and quality, theoretical and empirical, humility and self-confidence, individual and collective, practical and poetic, objective and subjective, artistic and technical, etc. Creativity involves locating a point of balance in this dynamic system, because it is there that you will find the tools to solve complex problems. It is the privilege of architects to be able to use their flexible way of thinking and *simultaneously* have the ability to use the linear thought, as needed.

Uncertainties are an integral and necessary part of the creative process, along with all the ethical/aesthetic, objective and subjective choices that vary from one project to the next. The process of criticism in architectural education helps in managing uncertainties by introducing and reinforcing criteria that make all these choices easier. If used properly, criticism has the potential to strengthen the students' individual, independent, creative relationship to their projects and the world around them. In the final analysis, it is the individual student's development that is important, because as Professor Keen Dorst puts it:

> *The art of design is linked to the designer, the design problem and the design situation, not just to the process of designing.* (Dorst 2006, 75)

This book was originally written in Swedish. Because of this, a pear plays an important role in the final chapter, since pears are namely an ingredient in the popular Swedish idiom Apples and Pears, and anything else is foreign. Nevertheless, since my translator explained that the corresponding expression in American English is Apples and Oranges, I suggest that the reader:

1 Accept the lecture as it was originally given at the start of my teaching career.

2 Amuse yourself afterwards by putting a different fruit in place of the pear and see where that leads you.

Apples and Pears (part of a lecture)

When you come, as I did, to another country, everything is interesting and new. I remember, during my early time in Sweden, feeling like I was in a fog of incomprehension. The Swedish language was like a flowing river. The intonation and the word stress were so different that I could not even tell where one sentence ended and the next began.

My first job was as a trainee at the big architectural office of the Swedish Cooperative Union. We used to eat our lunch in the staff cafeteria where I would sit at a long table with several others. It was interesting to listen to their unintelligible language, especially when I started to understand a little and I noticed that certain words were repeated in their conversations. For example, I could discern the word "anxiety" without knowing what it meant. I had never heard a corresponding word in my everyday Polish mother tongue, even if the term certainly existed in the medical vocabulary. The expression "it cost money" was also remarkable. It was so extraordinarily powerful; in Polish you would simply say that something costs a lot, or that it was a lot of money, but "it costs money"?

In my catalog of discoveries, I had also picked up the expression
"you shouldn't compare apples and pears". I thought that was pretty
funny. So imagine how surprised I was when the same phrase
popped up during a doctoral seminar a few years later, when
a professor emphatically corrected a doctoral candidate by exclaiming,
"you cannot compare apples and pears, you must never compare
apples and pears!". It suddenly became seductive, like most of the
things you really shouldn't do.

What happens if I do it?

What would happen if I were to compare apples and pears?

It is obvious that such a forbidden comparison intensely sharpens
my senses, my feeling of being in the moment is heightened.
I sense the freshness and sweetness…
My eyes see the disparity of form…the silhouettes have different
contours…the skins have dissimilar colors…
I imagine the tastes, fresh versus sour/sweet, and I feel the consist-
ency in my mouth…a touch would reveal the smoothness of the
apple and the slight friction on the skin of the pear…
it takes commitment to bite the apple… it releases an energetic
sound, quite different than the squish of the pear.

It is clear that the form gives me a lot of information. I can say that the apple is beautiful but not the pear, or vice versa. My judgment is entirely subjective and probably different than many others'. For instance, people have different abilities to see colors—and we even experience tastes differently. There can also be differences depending on what symbolic meanings we put upon our judgments. Immediately I see that the apple has great symbolism: not just as temptation for Adam and Eve in paradise, but also as a symbol of royal authority, apple-cheeked children, the happy family's apple pie, the hunger for knowledge in the form of a bitten apple. And if the legend is true, the falling apple that inspired Isaac Newton to discover the law of gravity.

In terms of the pear, the situation is difficult. I can only think of one, fairly vulgar, comparison of a pear to a body part. Otherwise, you could find a pear interesting because of its under-utilized symbolic potential. But in any event, I know what I think and feel about apples and pears, but does that apply to anyone else?

What is beautiful? What is ugly?

What is beautiful? What is ugly?

This is a question that has been asked many times in history and the erudite have debated whether beauty can be defined objectively or if it is something subjective.

(Subjective) Socrates felt that beauty was partly subjective and partly objective. There are things that are beautiful by themselves

and things that are beautiful for those who use them. He considered an object's usability to be very important.
(Objective) Plato maintained that beauty resides in the object; that there are things that are simply beautiful by themselves.

(S) Skeptics and Epicureans emphasized subjectivity.
(O) Plotinus said that there are things that are beautiful but not combined as objects: sun, light, gold….Beauty is not just elegant proportions, but also magnificent radiance.

(O) In the Middle Ages, the teachings of Augustine represented the objective viewpoint, while
(S) Thomas Aquinas thought that beauty was not an attribute, but instead a relationship between the subject and the object.

(O) During the Renaissance, Alberti placed great faith in objectivity: it is ignorant to maintain that the beauty of a building can change according to the viewer's taste and preferences, while
(S) Giordano Bruno pointed out that there is not a single thing that everyone can like.

(S) In the Baroque Europe of the 17th century, Spinoza stated that beauty is not a trait of the object, but instead a person's reaction to an object. There are no inherently beautiful or ugly things.
(S) Positivism was based on faith in verified knowledge, facts. This could not be applied to art. Gradually, a belief that beauty is solely a psychological phenomenon became adopted. The focus of the discussion shifted to determining which was more important: the form or the content. There were also different opinions about that.

I can try to investigate pears and apples in an objective way:
I slice through them with a sharp blade. Now I see the interior;
I can count and measure the seeds, compare their cores.

I can make a new cut and see what is revealed and another and
another, to a point where I don't know what is what.

Perhaps geometry could help me find some standard values?
In the sliced apple, I can inscribe both a square and a triangle.
A plethora of the symbolic numbers of Ancient Greece immediately
comes to mind.

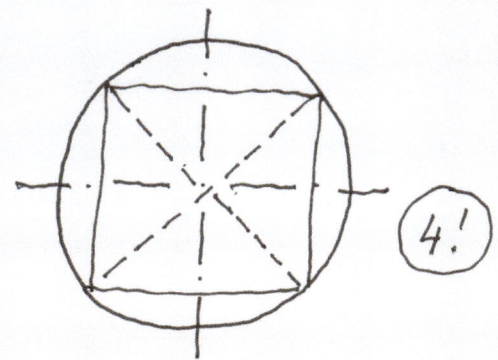

4!

1, 2, 3, 4 tetractys

$1 + 2 + 3 + 4 = 10$

$1^3 + 2^3 + 3^3 + 4^3 = 10^2$

10 = life
beauty
wordly perfection

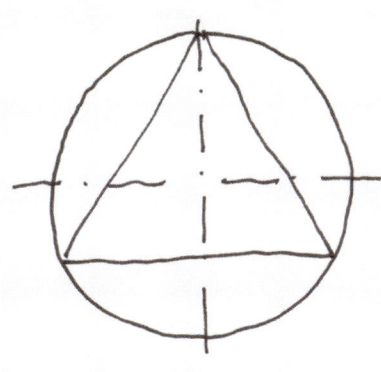
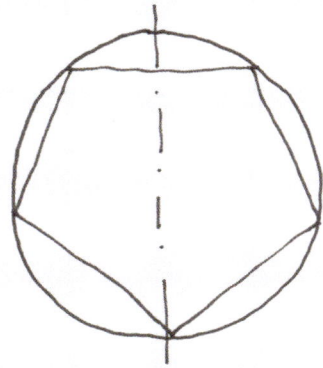

PYTHAGOREAN SCHOOL
approx. 500 BC
beauty = harmony
harmony = order
order = proportion/ratio
proportion/ratio =
                measure
measure = number

PROPORTION IS THE FOUNDATION OF BEAUTY

I do the same operation on the pear, checking proportions.

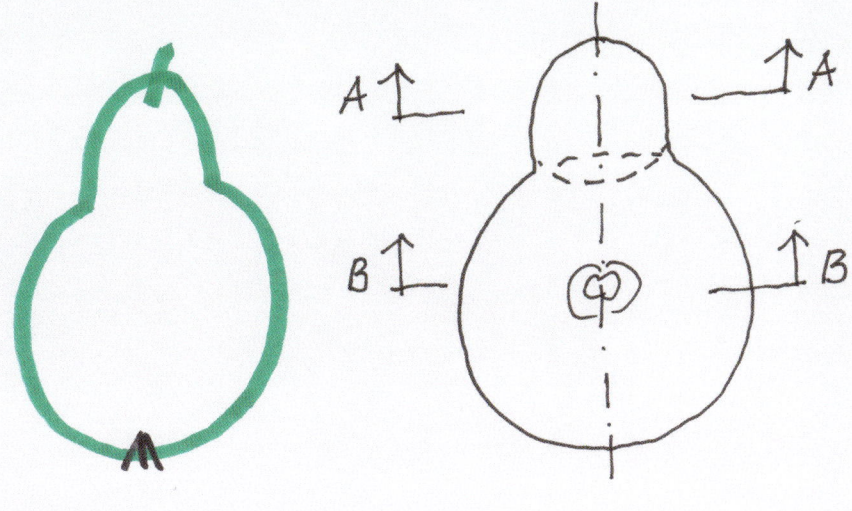

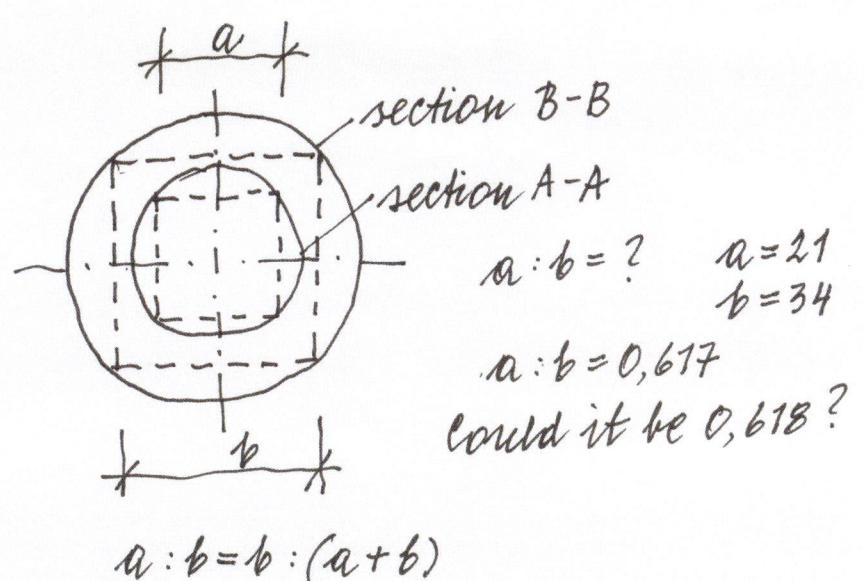

section B-B

section A-A

$a : b = ?$ $a = 21$
                $b = 34$

$a : b = 0{,}617$

could it be 0,618?

$a : b = b : (a + b)$

could it really be 0,618?!!!

Can it really be true? Is the legendary golden ratio the pear's silent revenge on the apple?

That may not be true, but nature does depend on order and laws and is therefore a great source of inspiration. This is emphasized by architects in certain periods. In other periods, sensory impressions can take over. Reflecting on what is subjective, what is objective, and everything in between can perhaps give me a compass to navigate through harmony and disharmony to a magnificent radiance.

Notes

References

1 The latter was shown in documents at the exhibition L'Italia di Le Corbusier at the MAXXI art museum in Rome 2012/2013.
2 The importance of social and ecological innovation is emphasized in various ways, for instance, by the Ruth and Ralph Erskine Nordic Foundation Prize.

Abitare A 487, 2008

Abitare A 491, 2009

Collins, Peter: *Architectural Judgement.* Faber & Faber, London 1971, 41

Dorst, Kees: *Understanding Design.* Gingko Press 2006, 75

Fisher, Thomas: *Ethics for Architects. 50 Dilemmas of Professional Practice.* Princeton Architectural Press, New York 2010

Fisher, Thomas: *Ethics. A Pervasive and Often Overlooked Presence in Architecture Education.* In: Ockman, Joan (ed.): *Architecture School. Three Centuries of Educating Architects in North America*, MIT Press 2012, 313–315

Fuller, R. Buckminster: *Education Automation. Comprehensive Learning for Emergent Humanity.* Lars Müller Publishers 2010 (1962)

Lawson, Bryan: *How Designers Think. The Design Process Demystified* (4th edn). Architectural Press 2008, 4, 55–73

Nussbaum, Martha: *The Discernment of Perception: An Aristotelian Conception of Private and Public*

Rationality. In: Nussbaum, Martha
C.: *Love´s Knowledge. Essays on
Philosophy and Literature.* Oxford
University Press 1990, 54–71

Ockman, Joan (ed.): *Architecture
School. Three Centuries of Educating
Architects in North America*, MIT
Press 2012

Papanek, Victor: *Design for the
Real World: Human Ecology and
Social Change*, Pantheon Books,
New York 1971

Popper, Karl: *Popper i urval av
David Miller.*
Stiftelsen Bokförlaget Thales 1997, 128

Sudjic, Deyan: *The Edifice Complex.
How the Rich and Powerful Shape the
World.* The Penguin Press. New York
2005, 8–15

Tatarkiewicz, W.: *Dzieje szesciu pojec.*
Panstwowe Wydawnictwo Naukowe,
Warszawa 1976

Zumthor, Peter: *Thinking Architecture.*
Lars Müller Publishers 1998, 9, 20–21

Zumthor, Peter: *Atmospheres.
Architectural Environments.
Surrounding Objects.* Birkhäuser –
Publishers for Architecture,
Basel 2006

Illustration credits

Personified geometry Riesch, G.: Margarita philosophica (Basle 1583) in Lawlor: *Sacred Geometry*, p.7 by permission of Thames and Hudson, **21** Examples of models by students in year 2, courtesy of Katarina Krupinska **33** Villa Savoye, photo: Christian Ahlskog **36** Turning Torso in Malmö, courtesy of Sture Samuelsson **63** Palazetto della sport, photo: the author **64** François Hennebique's own house, courtesy of Archive, The School of Architecture KTH **67** Lingotto Fiat factory in Torino, photo: the author **68** Guarino Guerini's dome from *The Projective Cast*: Architecture and Its Three Geometries, by Robin Evans, p. 362, © 1995 Massachusetts Institute of Technology, by permission of The MIT Press **68** The school in Paspels, courtesy of Heinrich Helfenstein **70** The extension of the Ordrupgaard Museum, ©Roland Halbe Architekturfotografie **72** The extension of the Ordrupgaard, a sketch, courtesy of Zaha Hadid Architects **73** The extension of the Ordrupgaard Museum, courtesy of Helen Binet **74** Street furniture, courtesy of Carolina Krupinska **77** Isometric perspective by Arne Jacobsen, courtesy of Danish National Art Library **80** "8TALLET" housing, photo by the author **83** The pocket watch by Le Corbusier, Fondation Le Corbusier, ©F.L.C. /BUS 2013 **93** The Wittgenstein House, photo: the author **95** Spatial studies, photo: the author **104** Tree hotel, Harads, photo: Åke E:son Lindman, courtesy of Tham & Videgård Arkitekter **112, 113** Townhouses, photo: Sune Sundahl, courtesy of Arkitektur- och designcentrum, Stockholm **128** Stadelhofen Railway Station, courtesy of Jesús Azpeita Seron **132** The stair at Joseph, Sloane Street, Richard Bryant/arcaid.co.uk **148** The stair at Boodles, Richard Bryant/arcaid. co.uk **149** New Museum of Contemporary Art, photo: Dean Kaufman, courtesy of SANAA **153** Rolex Learning Center, photo: SANAA, courtesy of SANAA **154** Interior of the MAXXI Museum, photo: Roland Halbe Architekturfotografie **157** MAXXI Museum, a sketch by Zaha Hadid, courtesy of Zaha Hadid Architects **157** A fishing bridge on Myrbærholmen, photo: Beate Hølmebakk, courtesy of Manthey Kula Architects **205** School of Architecture, the facade facing the city, courtesy of Carolina Krupinska **222** School of Architecture, courtesy of Carolina Krupinska **222** Proposal no. 1, sketch, courtesy of Dzenis Dzihic **225** Proposal no. 1, reworked, courtesy of Dzenis Dzihic **228–229** Proposal no. 1, the facade (skin), courtesy of Dzenis Dzihic **229** "The Path of Randomness"—a thesis project, rendering, courtesy of Anders Berg **257** Examples of plaster models, courtesy of Lennart Johansson **258** An apple and a pear, courtesy of photographer Charlie Bennet **269** Sliced fruits, courtesy of photographer Charlie Bennet **273** Geometry of an apple, sketch: author **275** Geometry of a pear, sketch: author **277**

Longer versions of the two essays that are published here—"Humble Assertiveness" and "A summer reflection"—may be found in the magazine *Arkitektur,* no. 7/1989 and in the *Yearbook 1998*, School of Architecture, The Royal Institute of Technology (KTH).

Index

Numbers in *italics* refer
to illustrations.